D1560190

MBO
for Nonprofit Organizations

MBO
for Nonprofit Organizations

Dale D. McConkey

A DIVISION OF AMERICAN MANAGEMENT ASSOCIATIONS

(

Library of Congress Cataloging in Publication Data

McConkey, Dale D
    MBO for nonprofit organizations.

    Bibliography: p.
    Includes index.
    1. Corporations, Nonprofit—Management.
2. Management by objectives.   I. Title.
HD38.M27   658'.04'8   75-25656
ISBN 0-8144-5379-1

Fourth Printing

This book is dedicated to the thousands of men and women who are currently making their contribution to better management in the nonprofit sector.

Preface

The conception of this book probably occurred during the early 1960s when I was prevailed upon (conned into would be more accurate) to accept the chairmanship of the community fund drive in a New England state. Almost immediately after my thankless appointment had been announced in the press, the heads of participating agencies started telling me just how much money they would like me to allocate to them from the proceeds of the coming drive. Many of these requests were masterpieces of brevity; for example, "Because of the expanded activities planned by our agency for next year, we will require $100,000 instead of the $75,000 we received last year. Your cooperation in raising this amount will be appreciated."

Possibly because I was an executive in a major corporation I thought those requests were a little too brief for the amount of funds being requested. Also, I concluded this was an unbusinesslike way to allocate the contributions collected from the public.

Within the next couple of weeks I informed each participating agency that all contributions would be disbursed in the following manner:

No agency would be promised a specific amount.

Each agency would be required to submit a comprehensive report of what it intended to accomplish (its objectives) and how much it would require to achieve those objectives.

The head of each agency would be required to appear personally before the community fund committee to justify his objectives and the monies requested.

Only after the above steps had been satisfactorily completed would the committee allocate monies to the agencies.

To say that the letter was received by the agencies as an act of pure heresy on my part would be an understatement. Comments from the agencies ranged from "He doesn't trust us" to "Who the hell does he think he is" to "He's calling us crooks." The stipulations in the letter were adhered to in the face of verbal flak and continuous pressure, and the funds were disbursed accordingly. The amount of monies received by many of the agencies differed markedly from the proportion of the amount they had received by the past "ask and ye shall receive" method. Major effort was devoted to allocating the funds on the basis of the needs to be met, the manner in which the needs would be met, and the degree to which both the needs and the manner of meeting them were justified by the agencies.

My experience was the beginning of what was to later develop into a major interest in improving the management of nonprofit organizations. In a very real sense, it provided the subject for this book and started my interest in writing it.

The intent of this book, then, is to bring to managers in the nonprofit sector the knowledge and intimate workings of a practical, proven system of management—management by objectives (MBO). The book goes into considerable detail about the components, operations, and applications of the MBO system. It shows, step by step, how the system can be applied to a nonprofit organization and its managers. Actual examples and MBO applications from many representative organizations in the nonprofit sector are included to demonstrate how MBO can and does improve organizational and managerial effectiveness.

I hope that the book will be of benefit to the thousands of

dedicated managers in the nonprofit sector as they strive to better carry out their mandate and stewardship.

I am indebted to many people whose help made this book possible. I am particularly grateful to the following individuals for their contributions of the case study chapters: Norman C. Allhiser, chairman of the Department of Business and Management, the University of Wisconsin at Madison, for the case study on the Management Institute; Robert C. Gronbach, assistant administrator of Hartford Hospital; Reverend Benjamin A. Gjenvick, executive director of Lutheran Social Services, for the case study on his organization; J. S. Hodgson, Deputy Minister of the Canadian Department of Veterans Affairs, for the case study on his department; and to several top administrators of the Public Health Service of the U.S. Department of Health, Education, and Welfare, for the case study on HEW.

A few passages in this book appeared previously in various publications and are reprinted with the permission of the original publishers. My thanks go to the editors of *Business Horizons,* Indiana University; *Management Review,* American Management Associations; *The Business Quarterly,* York University, Toronto, Canada; *The MBO Journal,* Classified Media Limited, London; and *Advanced Management Journal* of the Society for the Advancement of Management.

My thanks and appreciation also go to my secretary, Miss Mary A. Vance, for her typing and administrative work and to Mrs. Terri A. Buechner for her assistance with the typing. Thanks, Terri and Mary.

DALE D. McCONKEY

Contents

MBO
for Nonprofit Organizations

Introduction

The next major breakthrough in management will not occur in the corporate boardroom, nor will it have a business orientation. It won't even occur in the world of business.

The breakthrough will, and must, take place in the so-called nonprofit sector. We are presently seeing the beginnings of this breakthrough. The full impact of the breakthrough will become evident when there is general acceptance—one that is translated into practice—of the fact that a manager is a manager and that the demands upon him are the same, regardless of the product, service, or purpose of his organization. The pressure for accepting this fact is mounting most dramatically. It's been a long time coming!

Historically, we have been sadly negligent and often outright reluctant in emphasizing managerial effectiveness in the nonprofit sector. Effectiveness has been looked upon as being required almost exclusively of private-sector managers required to grub for the almighty buck. The purpose of many nonprofit organizations has been viewed as so laudable and high as to be above any consideration of effectiveness. As a natural consequence, persons with little or no management training have been hired, appointed, or promoted into positions requiring them to manage physical, capital, and human resources of a magnitude that would stagger even the better-trained and more competent managers in the private sector.

Management of nonprofit organizations has no landed right to be ineffective, to ignore managerial productivity, to ignore the "profit" motive, or to fail to evaluate new or revised approaches to management. Nor should the managers of these organizations be immune from strict accountability to those they serve, those upon whom they depend for their funds and support.

Nonprofit organizations, too, must earn a "profit" by operating with as much efficiency and effectiveness as possible to achieve the right priorities. While the nature of their profits may bear different labels, the profit motive must be present if they are to avoid economically and socially wasteful practices that raise major questions about their reason for being.

The Breakthrough

The continuing acceleration of two major forces will hasten the day when this next breakthrough in management takes place.

The first of these two forces is the unprecedented demand for stricter accountability for nonprofit managers. Owners, taxpayers, contributors, and others upon whom these organizations depend for their livelihood and existence are demanding proof of the results that nonprofit managers are achieving. Taxpayers are increasingly critical of the questionable effectiveness of government at all levels. Church members are asking how well the church is carrying out its stewardship. Volunteer organizations are no longer able to raise funds by merely championing the virtues of their cause. Social agencies are being required to demonstrate concrete ways by which they are meeting a need. Hospitals and health care agencies also are feeling the brunt of the demand for stricter accountability. In short, "accountability" has become a popular word in the nonprofit sector.

The second force operating in behalf of better management in the nonprofit sector is the sheer weight of numbers. Compared to business organizations, the proportionate growth of the nonprofit sector has been spectacular. In government alone, the increase in employment was a whopping 84 percent during the period 1955 to 1972. Federal civilian employment increased by 20 percent in the past 12 years. While the federal employment level has tended to flatten out during the past few years, this flattening is in marked contrast with the steep increase in state and local government employment. Total employment at the state and local level in 1974 totaled about 14 million people—up from 6 million in 1954.

Government purchases of goods and services now account for about 22 percent of the gross national product in the United States. This compares with 13 percent in 1950 and 10 percent in 1930. One out of every six American workers is a government employee, and estimates by the Bureau of Labor Statistics indicate that within the next decade one out of every four jobs will be a government job. Estimates project a 30 percent increase in state and local government employment by 1985.

Total cumulative federal expenditures from 1789 to 1849 approximated $1 billion. In 1950, they totaled $43 billion and in 1960, $92 billion. In 1973, these expenditures averaged about $1 billion for each working day.

The magnitude of the nonprofit sector in general becomes even more dramatic when one considers that 20 percent of the U.S. economy is in the nonprofit sector.

Growth of the entire "services" sector of the U.S. economy, of which nonprofit organizations are a major part, shows continuous increase. In 1870, services accounted for about 27 percent of total employment. This increased to 58 percent in 1970 and is projected to be more than 70 percent by the year 2000. In a world that is becoming more and more service-oriented, the growth of the nonprofit sector is not likely to diminish.

Toward a Viable Approach

The preponderance of management theory, philosophy, and practice is usually associated with industrial and business corporations, not with nonprofit organizations. By extension, it is quite popular to conclude that good management exists in the business world and poor management in the nonprofit sector. This polarization abounds in the minds of many people. It accounts to a large degree for many nonprofit managers becoming completely turned off when business management is discussed. This is unfortunate.

The managers of nonprofit organizations can gain much by objectively evaluating management practices that were tried and proven in business, and vice versa.

Whenever an overzealous businessman claims too many virtues for management of business corporations, the president of a community college well known for its management by objectives system shows him a popular study indicating that the overwhelming majority of business failures are attributable to managerial weaknesses.

One fruitful approach for promoting better management in the nonprofit sector is to examine the more successful business management practices and evaluate their potential applicability to nonprofit organizations. In his thought-provoking book, *Strategies for Survival,* David Linowes refers to the application of business management principles to nonprofit organizations, especially those in the public sector, as socio-economic management.[1] Linowes suggests ten principles of SEM for application to public organizations.

Tie standards and goals to proven human needs. The cost-effectiveness approach, which works so well for thousands of corporations, forces management to think through objectives and standards and to link them to proven needs.

Apply funding by results. How effectively are funds applied? Is a program fulfilling its purpose? How close to projected results did actual performance come?

Use discretionary funding as incentives. Discretionary funding as a means of recognizing outstanding performance would serve as a powerful stimulant to improved social profitability and, on the other hand, as a disincentive to penalize mediocrity.

Use multidisciplinary planning. The nonprofit manager should use all disciplines available—economics, business management, accounting, sociology, and so on—to help him manage his organization.

Set up social profitability audits. When billions of dollars of public funds are invested in social programs, the public is entitled to a qualitative evaluation of how the funds are being spent.

Establish public visibility. There should be full reporting to the public of the results achieved for the monies spent.

Prune and restructure for dynamic growth. The benefits of merging, divestiture, pruning, and restructuring are well under-

[1] AMACOM, 1973.

stood in the business community. The same approaches should be applied to social institutions and government agencies.

Vary the input mix. The businessman does not take profit for granted. He varies the input mix to continually improve performance. We must treat social programs as products with social values, and experiment with a variety of inputs to produce the best results.

Stir up social competition. Competitive sources of supply should be established for services provided. Let them compete with each other to provide the better services. Give the recipient a choice.

Fix responsibility for applying SEM. The agency or institution responsible for applying the principles of socio-economic management should be clearly established.

Linowes' recommendations are broad and far-reaching. But they go to the heart of many of the more pressing needs for better management in the nonprofit sector. Even more importantly from the standpoint of this book, the principles of SEM are consistent with and supportive of management by objectives (MBO) and its application to nonprofit organizations. Many of these principles are being practiced by the nonprofit organizations that have already implemented MBO.

Managing by Objectives

The question that plagues most managers, administrators, and executive personnel of nonprofit organizations is not whether they should become more effective but how the improvement can be brought about—what means, methods, or tools are available to them.

One of the approaches being used with increasing success is management by objectives (or management by results, as it also is termed). Although MBO developed and has realized its major success in businesses operating for profits, it is equally applicable and beneficial to the nonprofit organization.

In essence, MBO is a systematic approach to achieving desired ends. When viewed in this context, it is obvious that it has considerable value when applied to nonprofit organizations. Those who would hold otherwise place themselves in the untenable position of advocating that the desired end (for example, quality education) should be approached by hit-or-miss methods. No organization, profit or nonprofit, has a right to assume such a ridiculous position.

 Nonprofit organizations are not unique. Like all organizations, they have an objective to achieve; namely, to provide the highest quality product or service consistent with the funds available. Assets have been entrusted to them—people, capital, and plant and equipment. They serve in a stewardship capacity to those upon whom they depend for their continued existence. Managers of these organizations have no inherent right to waste any of these assets or to violate their stewardship. These managers, too, must be held accountable for results.

Highly successful MBO applications have been made in every conceivable type of organization—profit and nonprofit, large and small—in the private and public sectors and in the United States, Canada, Europe, Japan, and elsewhere. These include hospitals, schools, police departments, nursing homes, defense departments, municipal government units, and agencies of federal governments. Nursing homes, churches, and child-care centers all have embraced MBO, as have many other nonprofit organizations. On the basis of the experience to date, it appears only logical that nonprofit applications will continue and will accelerate.

Applicability to Nonprofit Organizations

Those who might question the applicability of MBO to nonprofit organizations would do well to answer the following questions. The questions cover the major aspects of organizing and managing an operation. Also, the questions exert the major impact on MBO and, in turn, MBO exerts a major impact on them:

1. Does the organization have a mission to perform? In other words, is there a valid reason for it to exist?
2. Does management have assets (money, people, plant and equipment) entrusted to it?
3. Is management accountable to some person or authority for a return on the assets?
4. Can priorities be established for accomplishing the mission?
5. Can the operation be planned?
6. Does management believe it must manage effectively even though the organization is a nonprofit one?
7. Can accountabilities of key personnel be pinpointed?

8. Can the efforts of all key personnel be coordinated into a whole?
9. Can necessary controls and feedback be established?
10. Is it possible to evaluate the performance of key personnel?
11. Is a system of positive and negative rewards possible?
12. Are the main functions of a manager (planning, organizing, directing, and so on) the same regardless of the type of organization?
13. Is management receptive to improved methods of operating?

The reader might conclude that these are loaded questions. They are! It is all but impossible to answer "no" to any of them. Answering "no" places the manager in the position of advocating ineffective management. Yet, taken together, the subject matter of these questions does an excellent job of describing what MBO is all about—namely, managing resources to achieve economically significant results.

Most nonprofit organizations are starving for better management methods, and much of this hunger is caused by increasing pressures from those who use their services and those who finance their endeavors. Given this situation, even an MBO system whose full impact cannot be realized immediately because of special circumstances, discussed in Chapter 3, would appear eminently better than continuing to waste away as the hunger remains unsatiated.

At the same time, MBO will help to quickly spot limitations or special considerations so that all possible action can be taken to eliminate or minimize them. In the absence of MBO the limitations are destined to continue, often without recognition of their impact on the progress of the organization. Concurrently, the organization's valuable resources continue to be dissipated. It often is said that much of problem solving results from properly identifying and defining the problem; one of the chief virtues of MBO is its ability to highlight sacred cows and other impediments to increased effectiveness.

Today, MBO is making rapid strides in nonprofit organizations. While its progress has not been as dramatic or widespread as is true with business firms, it is becoming increasingly difficult to find a category of nonprofit organization in which MBO has not been successfully applied.

Over 20 years of MBO experience has demonstrated the value

and applicability of MBO to all types of organizations. The non-profit sector is no exception. This same experience has demonstrated that MBO can be applied to these organizations only if they insist upon and meet the same demands that the system imposes upon other categories of endeavors. As a minimum these demands include:

1. The selection of highly competent managers, administrators, and professionals for all key positions.

2. In-depth training in the complete MBO system before any attempt is made to apply it.

3. Allowing the three to four years required for successful implementation.

4. Substitution of maximum participation from all personnel for the sometimes autocratic and despotic decisions of a few.

5. Complete tailoring of the MBO system to the individual problems or conditions existing in the individual organization.

6. The removal, or diminishing, by legislative or executive action impediments to the ability of MBO to achieve its full potential—such as emphasizing effort rather than results, provisions that protect ineffective personnel, practices that stifle individual initiative and lead to inflexible decision making, and systems that fail to provide recognition and rewards.

7. Constant reexamination of the system after installation to improve it and render it responsive to changing conditions.

MBO cannot be blamed for any problems resulting from management's failure to meet these exhaustive and exhausting demands. The blame for any difficulties must be placed squarely upon the shoulders of the real culprits—the persons who fail to meet the demands that the system imposes or who fail to adapt it to the circumstances existing in their organizations.

DISCUSSION CASE
Your Organization Is Not Unique

It is sometimes said that better management techniques are difficult or impossible to apply to many nonprofit organizations. For example, many people have said that New York City is not manageable because of its size and multiplicity of problems.

Often, we tend to believe that the uniqueness of our organization, or imposed limitations, makes it impossible to adopt new management practices. These limitations can be real or imagined. Our task becomes one of separating the real from the imagined.

DISCUSSION POINTS

1. Make a detailed list of the possible limitations that you believe exist in your organization.
2. Discuss each one in detail.
3. Weight each one from 1 to 5 on the basis of your ability to remove or work within the limitation ("5" represents the lesser limitation).
4. Plan how you can minimize the more significant limitations (those that you scored 3 or higher).

1

What Is MBO?

There are almost as many definitions of management by objectives (MBO) as there are writers, practitioners, and theoreticians who have concerned themselves with the subject. Thus the definitions run the gamut from two or three lines of oversimplification to many paragraphs of oversophistication. Hopefully, the following definition, which will be used throughout this book, represents a balance between the two extremes. I do not intend this as the ultimate definition but rather as one that will provide the reader with the necessary guidance for understanding the MBO system of managing. Here is my definition:

> MBO is a systems approach to managing an organization—*any* organization. It is not a technique, or just another program, or a narrow area of the process of managing. Above all, it goes far beyond mere budgeting even though it does encompass budgets in one form or another.
>
> First, those accountable for directing the organization determine where they want to take the organization or what they want it to

achieve during a particular period (establishing the overall objectives and priorities).

Second, all key managerial, professional, and administrative personnel are required, permitted, and encouraged to contribute their maximum efforts to achieving the overall objectives.

Third, the planned achievement (results) of all key personnel is blended and balanced to promote and realize the greater total results for the organization as a whole.

Fourth, a control mechanism is established to monitor progress compared to objectives and feed the results back to those accountable at all levels.

The Key Word

Contrary to popular thinking, the key word in the term "management by objectives" is not the word "objectives" but the word "management." Again, this is a necessary and important distinction. The failure to appreciate this distinction has been at the root of many of management's failures in attempting to practice MBO.

The following sequence of events usually occurs when "objectives" is considered the key word. First, and generally, objectives are overemphasized in relation to the system. Second, the setting of objectives becomes a fetish. Third, managers are required to write a list of objectives for their jobs. Those objectives are commonly written in a vacuum, without completion of the necessary preliminary action that must precede the objectives. The result to the manager is a list of uncoordinated and unbalanced objectives whose meaning, importance, and function seem incomprehensible. Often, the manager is puzzled as to how the objectives can help him manage his job better. Actually, objectives written in this manner can impede rather than aid job performance.

The successful MBO manager views objectives as only one part—admittedly a vitally important part—of a total system. He insures that the management system is in place so that he can position objectives into the system rather than have them stand on their own and see them as the system. The manager must first master the system—determine what it is, what it isn't, its rationale, the prerequisites to be met, the pitfalls to be wary of, the mechanics of the system, the components. Then, and only then, does he address himself to objectives proper. The system and its components are examined in detail later in this chapter.

The Definition in Practice

The MBO system begins with the establishment of overall objectives for the total organization for the target period. In the Department of Defense, one of the overall objectives might be to attain a stipulated level of defense readiness or capability. Once the top management of the organization has established these overall objectives, they constitute the sum total of the results that must be accomplished by all the managers of that organization; that is, at the end of the target period, the total of the results accomplished by all the managers must add up, as a minimum, to the overall objectives that were set earlier.

MBO is adaptable to any type of organization as long as that organization has a mission to perform. The only difference is that the type and content of the objectives will differ. In a police department, the objective may be to lower the crime rate to a stipulated level. In a school system, the objective might be to provide specific educational benefits at various cost levels. The overall objective for a charitable institution might be to provide a certain level of assistance. The objective for an air defense fighter squadron probably would be to engage the enemy within a specified period after receiving an alert.

Once the top objectives have been approved, the next step is to translate them into the required action each manager in the organization must take. The objective-setting process is complete when each of the managers—both line and staff and at all levels from top management down to and including the lowest-level manager—has objectives that, when added up, will at least equal the overall objectives of the enterprise. Another way to describe MBO is that it is the full, in-depth delegation of pieces of the overall organizational objectives down the line so that each manager is accountable for accomplishing part of the higher-level objectives.

The Systems Approach

MBO can be referred to as a systems approach to managing an organization. The "systems" nature of the approach as it is presently practiced becomes clear when we delve into the definit.... of a system that I'll describe as being a combination of actions (or components) that, when acting as a whole, cause something to happen. The components of an electric doorbell are a good example of a system and its operation. The components in this case are a power source (electricity), a conducting medium (electrical wire), a triggering mechanism (the button), and an action vehicle (the bell mechanism). All four components must be present and must play their proper role if the desired action—the ringing of the bell—is to take place. In the case of MBO the system comprises:

Objectives
Plans
Managerial direction and action
Control (monitoring)
Feedback

The absence of any one of these key components of the MBO system will render it inoperative. In the early days of MBO there was often a lack of one, two, or even more of the key components. For example, it has long been fashionable to uphold the virtue and use of objectives and an even cursory review of literature will reveal the extensive adoption of objectives on a wide scale. As we shall see later, the quality and value of the early objectives were subject to considerable criticism. But until recently, there was a glaring lack of one of the other key components that must always accompany objectives if they are to be accomplished—the plans for making them work. The inherent defects in the type of objectives formerly used and the lack of plans for accomplishing them resulted in major weaknesses in the other components of the system— managerial direction and action, control and feedback.

The Emergence of MBO as a System

Before MBO could emerge as a system it was necessary to correct these weaknesses by strengthening each component and meshing each improved component into a smoothly working, effective whole.

Objectives. Typically, objectives were formerly little more than general statements of management's wishes. It was not uncommon to find objectives such as:

Achieve the greatest possible cost/benefit ratio for all tax dollars collected.

Run our organization in the most efficient manner possible.

Provide the highest-quality services to our patients.

Insure a meaningful learning experience for our students.

All these wishes are laudable and because they are, they became known as "Motherhood" objectives. However, they did little, if anything, to fulfill the basic requirements of meeting objectives. They did not provide concrete directions to managers in that they didn't tell them what must be accomplished, how much must be accomplished, who was to accomplish it, or when it must be accomplished.

MBO required that objectives be removed from the general, nebulous, blue-sky thinking category into a new category in which they would be specific and measurable and thus would provide proper direction for all the managers in an organization. This was accomplished by applying the "3Ws": What will be done? When will it be done? Who will do it?

With the advent of specific, time-limited, and clearly delineated objectives we began to witness the beginnings of the systems approach. The word "beginnings" is used advisedly because it remained to formulate concrete plans for accomplishing the specific objectives.

Plans. Prior to MBO as it is presently practiced, it was an all-too-frequent practice for organizations to structure their objectives, even highly specific ones, and then fail to develop the concrete plans and actions that, when completed, would result in the accomplishment of the objectives. It seemed almost as if they were relying on the Almighty to see to it that the objectives did in fact get accomplished. MBO stopped this praying and wishing and substituted "backbone management" for "wishbone management."

The role of plans in MBO may be illustrated by a common objective for a hospital administrator: Achieve an average monthly occupancy rate of 78 percent during the year 1975.

To justify that this is a realistic and obtainable objective and to provide the means by which he will achieve it, this manager must develop concrete plans. These plans should include a statement of the step-by-step action he will pursue to achieve the objective.

Once his plans have been formulated, he must test them for reasonableness. Are the plans as realistic as he can make them? Has sufficient justification been included with respect to his assumptions and alternatives? Have all possible alternatives been considered? Do the plans contain any unjustified or blue-sky thinking? Will the plans hold up under a penetrating analysis? If the plans come true as written, is it reasonable to expect that the objective will be achieved?

Managerial direction and action. The next component of the MBO system requires the manager to give proper direction and take action to accomplish what the company wishes to achieve—in other words, to carry out his objectives and plans. This component includes major functions such as organizing, communicating, motivating, coordinating, and developing subordinates. It brings to life the objectives and plans the manager established; it's the action vehicle of MBO.

Control (monitoring). Returning again to the conditions existing prior to MBO, we find that management's control function was largely inadequate and going through its infancy. Controls were either too general or, when they were specific, they were attempting to monitor nonspecific matters. Consequently, the controls did not serve their intended purpose. Control was largely an after-the-fact reporting of what actually happened as opposed to what someone thought *should* happen.

Under MBO a specific objective is decided upon first. Second, a specific control is tailored to measure the specific objective. In other words, we first determine where we want to go and then decide upon the one best method for determining whether or not we are getting there.

Another problem with controls as they were formerly used was that they were not designed to serve the differing needs of the various levels of management. Too frequently, control was considered as being necessary only at the upper levels of management but not really necessary at intermediate and lower levels. Under MBO each manager has controls for each of the objectives for which he is responsible, and these controls are tailored to his particular needs at his level.

As a very minimum, each control must include the objective (or subject matter) being measured, the method of measuring, the frequency of measuring, and to whom the control information will be sent.

Feedback. Control is useless unless the information is placed in the hands of those who must make the decisions and subsequently use the information to check the validity of their decisions and take appropriate corrective action when necessary. Thus we come to feedback and its part in the MBO system. Feedback requires that each manager receive the type of information, in the right form and at the right frequency, that he requires to carry out the accountabilities of his job. The manager need not be deluged with information; he need receive only that which he requires.

Figure 1 provides an excellent illustration and summary of the key components of the MBO system.

Figure 1. The elements of managing.

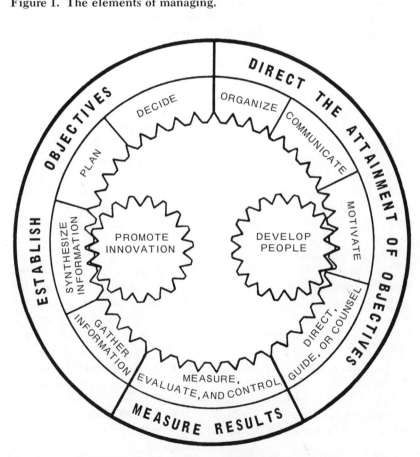

Source: BMC REPORT NUMBER 1, Business Management Council, New York, 1968.

DISCUSSION CASE
Where Does Your Organization Stand?

One of the more appropriate ways to view MBO is that it resulted from a concerted attempt to select the best of all known management approaches and combine these parts into one systematic, total way of managing an organization. Thus many organizations probably have been practicing certain aspects of the MBO system for many years. For example, objectives in one form or another have been used since biblical times, and many organizations already have budgets.

DISCUSSION POINTS

1. Which parts of the MBO system is your organization currently practicing?
2. What are the strong and weak points relative to those parts that you are currently practicing? Where is improvement necessary?
3. Which additional parts of the system would it be necessary to adopt if the total systems approach is to be followed?

2

Evolution and Current Status of MBO

As a system of managing, MBO was conceived in the world of business and so far has achieved its greatest impact in the private sector. Thus any discussion of the evolution of MBO must necessarily be addressed to the development of the system in corporations. However, the increasing adoption of MBO by nonprofit organizations within the past five years has started to build an additional body of MBO experience.

Although it is difficult to apply the description "milestone" to only some elements in a series of events, certain events can be singled out as the most significant in the evolution of MBO. The first milestone is the translation of the MBO concept into reality. Objectives of one variety or another have been known and used by managers since biblical times. It remained for Peter Drucker, writing in 1954, to utilize them as the basis for a management system.[1] Always the able catalyst to management thinking, Drucker

---

[1] *The Practice of Management* (New York: Harper & Row).

set the stage by proposing that objectives would serve as the vehicle for administering and directing a systems approach to managing an organization. Others would develop the system and render it operative. Approximately 20 years after Drucker's lucid pronouncement, MBO became a practical reality embodied, successfully and unsuccessfully, in thousands of various and diverse organizations throughout the world. Concept has been translated into practice.

The second milestone is the three-stage evolution of MBO from its fledgling stage to the present. Initially, almost complete emphasis was on improving the performance of the individual manager—by providing him with goals toward which to strive and by according him recognition for his achievements. Next, emphasis switched to the organization as a total entity, and the goal was overall organizational effectiveness on a short-range basis. Finally, the long-run future of the organization was emphasized by balancing and directing the results of individual managers to achieve organizational priorities.[2]

The third milestone was realized when MBO advanced from a special-purpose management tool or technique into a full-fledged management system.

The early efforts of the pioneers in MBO arose primarily from a complete disenchantment with the techniques then popular for evaluating or appraising managerial performance. The evaluation techniques of the late 1950s measured the degree to which managers were thought to possess, or to fail to possess, highly subjective traits or factors. Factors commonly evaluated were cost-awareness, grasp of function, initiative, innovation, punctuality, loyalty, cooperation, potential for advancement, and the like. The traits were not keyed to actual results achieved, and two evaluations of the same manager could differ by 180 degrees because of the orientation and prejudices of the examiners.

Gradually, measurable objectives and results replaced evaluations of traits. This required the development of effective objectives for managers, and here we see the beginnings of the new system. The development of objectives appropriate for use in evaluating performance paved the way for allowing objectives to serve as the focal point for all other major parts of the management process.

[2] See Robert A. Howell, "Managing by Objectives—A Three-Stage System," *Business Horizons*, February 1970, pp. 41–45.

Extent of Adoption

The precise extent to which MBO has been adopted is impossible to gauge. To date there is no valid data on the number of organizations that have adopted MBO. Any attempt to arrive at the number is complicated by the need for a definition of the degree of MBO that an organization must practice to qualify for inclusion in the statistics. Moreover, the collection of data would be further confused because of the uncertainty concerning what MBO is.

Some managers classify themselves as MBO practitioners simply because they operate with budgets. Others do so because they work with general goals and objectives, and others because they believe they are following a few MBO principles—as they understand them. And still others profess to be full-fledged MBO managers because they give their subordinates some voice in decision making.

The above variations notwithstanding, there is no question that MBO has been adopted extensively. Applications are found in abundance in large and small companies and in all areas of the business sector—in both capital-goods and consumer-goods companies and in companies with product lines as divergent as turbines and facial tissues and with goals as different as producing a product and providing a service.

The nonprofit sector, having witnessed the attention devoted to MBO in the private sector, has begun to adopt MBO at a rather startling pace. This trend is discernible among government units, in hospitals and the health-care field, among religious organizations, in educational systems, in volunteer organizations, and in practically all other areas of the nonprofit sector. Impetus from the highest offices of the federal governments in both the United States and Canada in 1973 and 1972, respectively, set the theme for increased adoption of MBO. Both of these governments mandated MBO as the way of managing federal departments. Much of this emphasis has, in turn, been translated to the state and provincial levels of government, especially in those state agencies that are dependent to one degree or another on federal funding.

Service organizations, whose growth is outpacing manufacturing entities, constitute another vital area of increased MBO application. Many insurance companies, banks, and retail establishments are presently exploring and adopting the MBO system.

A pattern of adoption within geographical locations is also evident. From the United States, MBO has spread to England, Europe, Japan, Canada, and other parts of the globe.

Thus MBO has been widely adopted and is being extensively practiced. This adoption is not based upon its proven value but upon its logical appeal. To date, there has been no validation through a representative sample of the degree to which MBO increases organizational or managerial effectiveness. However, it can be demonstrated, without attempting to quantify the results, that practicing MBO in depth does result in improved communication, coordination, control, and motivation of managers. These desirable ends are considered the minimum an organization should expect from its MBO efforts, and there is little if any disagreement that these benefits do accrue when MBO is employed for at least two to three years.

Before we proceed to a discussion of the specific changes MBO has helped bring about, the absence of "pure" MBO systems must be indicated. If pure MBO is defined as a system in which all the commonly accepted principles of MBO are practiced in A-to-Z fashion, few, if any, organizations actually practice MBO.

Major differences exist in the applications of MBO, both in the procedures for accomplishing the applications and in the degree of conviction with which MBO is pursued. For example, some organizations embrace the method primarily as a means of evaluating their managers, while others use it primarily for planning. Still others employ MBO as the overall management system. Even within different divisions of the same organization, there are considerable differences in the approach and applications.

Impact on Managing

The impact of MBO on the management process and on the manager has been profound and dramatic. Nowhere is this impact more demonstrable than in the change in the very definition of "management."

Formerly, if a person were asked to define management, he might reply, "It's getting things done through people." If pressed to amplify his definition, he might add "by planning, organizing, directing, and controlling." This rather common, traditional definition of management was rendered obsolete by a recent study completed by a committee of the Association of Consulting Management Engineers and reported by the Business Management

Council.[3] The study concluded that management comprises three steps: establishing objectives, directing the attainment of objectives, and measuring results.

The "management wheel" that resulted from the study was shown in Figure 1. The three major steps in managing are divided into their eleven elements. Thus, in lieu of defining management by general terms or by citing a list of functions that the manager carries out, management now is defined as comprising three major steps—all highly oriented toward objectives. Now the former main functions are subfunctions of the three larger steps. This change in emphasis and the rationale leading to the change have brought about far-reaching changes in many of the traditional approaches to the manager's job. Several of these key changes are described later.

Not the least of these changes has been the major distinction established between "running" an organization and "managing" it. Those who run an organization are usually frantically busy doing many different things, often working excessively long hours, and hoping that something will happen. Those who manage it make things happen by deciding what they should be doing and then lining up all their resources and actions to make it happen. The latter are usually in control of their operations; the former frequently have operations that are out of control.

Management Styles

Twenty years of MBO experience have demonstrated that MBO enjoys a better chance for success if its practitioners follow a particular management style. Experience has proved that MBO cannot be successfully foisted on the wrong management style. The entire management style and approach must be supportive of MBO or it will not reach its success potential. The more successful approaches have been those in which management can be characterized by a balanced, participative style, one that encourages maximum participation while discouraging permissiveness. For obvious reasons, MBO will be least successful with an autocratic management. While MBO can achieve some measure of success in a bureaucratic atmosphere, its effectiveness will be greatly decreased by the excess of red tape, controls, and procedures.

[3] *BMC Report Number 1*, Business Management Council, New York, 1968.

The balanced, participative style is usually defined as one in which the maximum number of the following attributes is actually practiced to the maximum degree:

There is in-depth delegation.
There is maximum participation in the objective-setting and planning processes.
Managers are permitted to make mistakes.
Change is encouraged and planned for.
Policies and procedures are minimal and subject to change when necessary.
Controls are tight, but only the minimum are imposed to keep the unit in control.
There is a meaningful reward system.
Managers exercise a high degree of self-management, self-discipline, and self-control.

Increased Use of Behavioral Sciences

More and more, MBO is raising the status of behavioral scientists from mere voices crying in the wilderness to valuable, recognized members of the management process. According to my concept, management thinking passed through three stages of development and is on its way to the fourth stage, the MBO system.

Stage 1. This stage was exemplified by the birth and adoption of the so-called scientific management approach. Stage 1 relied heavily on a more impersonal approach to managing people, and was characterized by emphasis on standards, work measurement, and methods improvement. Its leading advocates were Taylor and the Gilbreths.

Stage 2. A swing toward more attention to the human or personal factor in managing people, Stage 2 was a natural outgrowth of the emphasis on the impersonal approach. Much of the thinking of Stage 2 can be attributed to Elton Mayo and those who follow his work.

Stage 3. This stage can be described as an era of discontinuity. During this period a sizable chasm developed between the purists, frequently hard-nosed production managers who advocated the scientific management approach and regarded behavioral scientists as socialist theorizers, and the behavioral scientists, who often looked upon scientific managers as hard-core profit-seekers with inadequate appreciation for the human factor and the how and why of motivating people.

Stage 4. The end of Stage 3 came in the late 1950s. The move to participative management within the MBO system started a narrowing of the gap between impersonal and personal management approaches. MBO, while continuing to emphasize the importance of achieving the necessary objectives of the organization, also placed a premium on marshaling and directing all the human assets toward those objectives. Applications of the behavioral sciences were evident. This trend continues as MBO serves increasingly as a marrying agent.

Increasing Use of Staff Managers

Prior to MBO, the staff manager was frequently regarded as a necessary evil, as one who dealt with intangibles that could not be measured. Often he received neither the opportunity to make a contribution nor the acceptance and recognition for his accomplishments when they were achieved.

The advanced applications of MBO now permit staff managers to write measurable objectives, to measure rather finitely their contributions against their objectives, to receive deserved recognition in the process, and to take their proper place as members of the profit-making team. With staff managers currently constituting an increasingly higher percentage of an organization's total manpower budget, their increased utilization must be credited as being one of MBO's greater contributions. While some organizations have been slow to bring staff managers into the MBO system, the number that now consider staff managers as an integral part of MBO is steadily increasing.[4]

Appraising Managers

One of the most dramatic changes brought about by MBO has been its impact on measuring managerial performance. MBO has been instrumental in a three-stage progression concerning managerial appraisals.

Stage 1 (pre-MBO) was a period in which the emphasis was

[4] See Dale D. McConkey, *Management by Objectives for Staff Managers* (New York: Vantage Press, 1972).

Figure 2. History of approaches to managerial appraisal.

STAGE 1 Measuring by Traits Pre-MBO	STAGE 2 Measuring by Objectives 1955–1972	STAGE 3 Measuring by Objectives and Efficiency 1972–
Emphasis was on measuring managers based on trait factors, such as health, initiative, loyalty, punctuality, and grasp of function.	Emphasis was on measuring managers based on degree to which they achieved, or failed to achieve, their objectives.	Emphasis was on objectives and how efficiently managers achieved their objectives.
This was an extremely weak approach because it was not related to results which the manager achieved.	This was a much better approach as it was results-oriented. However, it emphasized effectiveness: were the objectives achieved or not? It failed to consider efficiency: was the achievement based on good management practices?	This has the added advantage of coupling effectiveness (were the objectives achieved?) with efficiency (did the manager accomplish the results by luck or by sound management?).

on measuring performance by rating traits; Stage 2 switched the emphasis to measurement based primarily on the achievement of preset objectives; Stage 3 concentrates on measures designed to evaluate managers both on the degree to which objectives are achieved and on how efficiently the objectives are achieved. Figure 2 highlights the major characteristics of each of the three stages.[5]

Job Description

MBO has all but eliminated the traditional job description, which catalogued what the company required of the *job*, not of the *manager* in the job. The emphasis in MBO descriptions is on the manager because the system recognizes that it is the man who makes the job in the managerial ranks (see Figure 3 for a comparison of the differences between the traditional and the MBO job description).

[5] For an in-depth discussion of the third stage, see Harold Koontz, *Appraising Managers as Managers* (New York: McGraw-Hill, 1972).

Figure 3. Comparison of traditional and MBO job descriptions.

	Traditional	MBO
Major thrust	Heavily oriented to long statements of activities.	Oriented to objectives.
Change factor	Seldom changes unless major function is added or subtracted from the job.	Objectives portion changes at least once each year.
Priorities	Lack of change precludes recognizing changing priorities.	Changing priorities are recognized through changing objectives.
Improvement	Lack of recognition of change precludes inclusion of improvement as a factor.	Continual improvement can be programmed into the changing objectives.
Orientation	Heavily job-tailored; frequently ignores the man and differences in men.	Man-tailored; individual strengths can be capitalized on.

It is not possible to overemphasize the importance of the document that describes the manager's accountability. This document serves as the basis for evaluating the manager's performance, for rewarding him, and for gauging the countless other actions related to individual performance. The sum of all these activities determines the future of the entity.

Compensation Practices

MBO has had a pronounced impact on compensation practices. Prior to the widespread adoption of MBO, it was quite common for compensation to be based on so-called merit principles. However, "merit" was a highly elusive term, and few organizations succeeded in realizing it in actual practice. Too often, for example, "merit" became synonymous with "longevity." Invariably, there was a tenuous connection between a manager's compensation and the contribution he made.

As often as not, compensation plans did everything possible to destroy the prime objectives of compensation: promoting equity and motivation. Rewards that were not tied to specific results—and were not given to the manager in proportion to the results he achieved—could hardly be considered equitable or a motivating force to encourage better performance. MBO had precipitated fun-

Figure 4. Comparison of old and new planning approaches.

	Static Planning (Old Way)	vs.	Dynamic Planning (New Approach)
Purpose	Get a "plan."		Achieve optimum results.
Basic premise	Forecasts are accurate.		Future is unpredictable.
Technique	Static, periodic.		Dynamic, continuous.
Process	Rigid, formal, pre-scribed.		Flexible, selective adaptation.
Management style	Traditional, authoritative.		Decentralized, participative.
Responsibility	Top management. VP, planning. Centralized planning staff.		Every manager. Director, planning services. Decentralized planning coordinators.
Types of planning Strategic Operational Logistic	Separate plans.		Integrated planning.
Functional planning Marketing Financial Personnel, and so on	Separate plans.		Integrated planning.
Time spans Short Medium Long-range	Separate plans.		Integrated planning.
Support	Resistance and resentment.		Enthusiastic participation.
Durability	Tapers off to discouragement.		Growing value and enthusiasm.
Cost/benefits	Too much time-effort-paper. Higher cost. Limited benefits.		Better decisions and programs. Less time and effort. Better results.

SOURCE: Edward J. Green, "The Communication Crisis," Marshall Allan Robinson lecture, University of Pittsburgh, 1972.

damental changes by insisting that compensation be tied closely to achievement of objectives and paid in proportion to the degree to which the objectives are achieved or exceeded.

Of at least equal importance in the rewards process, MBO has provided the possibility for recognizing contributions when promotion time arrives.

As will be seen in Chapter 3 considerable work remains to be done in nonprofit organizations to establish a more direct tie between objective results and compensation.

Planning

Probably no other aspect of the management process has received such a substantial jolt from MBO as planning has. Formerly, planning was an exercise in writing tolerated to satisfy the organization's requirements; now its value and help to the individual manager are increasingly appreciated. More important, the manager recognizes the real need for planning. He can appreciate its necessity.

Edward Green, one of the authorities in the area of corporate planning, has compared what he terms the traditional approach to planning with the more modern approach, which is markedly oriented toward MBO. Figure 4 (page 27) outlines Green's comparison.

Delegation

MBO has at last brought real meaning to the definition of delegation. Formerly, delegation was defined as "getting things done through other people." This wholly inadequate definition failed to recognize that "things" can be good, bad, or indifferent.

Now delegation is approached in a manner that is conducive to achieving more positive results. Under MBO, a subordinate is not told to go out and do something or to get things done. Instead, he is delegated specific objectives or end results for which he is accountable. Both he and his boss know the specific end results he must achieve.

One of the cardinal mandates of MBO is that the manager must have sufficient authority to accomplish his objectives. For the first time, in many instances managers are receiving clear definitions of the authority they may exercise. Statements such as "He shall enjoy authority commensurate to carry out his job" are rapidly giving way to rather finite statements.

The impact of MBO on the overall management process, and especially its effect on delegation, has provided a viable foundation for the practice of participative management. When specific objectives have been delegated to the individual manager, he can determine much of his own destiny—he can help set his objectives, do much of his own planning to achieve those objectives, operate with the authority he knows he has, and take the initiative when corrective action is required. The emphasis on delegating end results permits participation and helps considerably in preventing permissive management.

In an era in which one of the popular buzzwords is "job enrichment"—with attention so far directed almost exclusively to the employee instead of to the manager—MBO has made considerable strides in enriching the manager's job. The practice of MBO in depth culminates in each manager's becoming head of his own suborganization. When this end is reached, the manager experiences substantial job enrichment because his destiny depends largely upon his own efforts.

Decision Making

The decision-making process also has come in for its share of change as a result of MBO. Two aspects of MBO have helped bring about this change. The first is the feedback and data, tailored and directed to the individual manager; the second is the structuring of strict accountability for each manager.

Feedback. Advocates of decentralization have long maintained that decisions should be made at the lowest possible level of management at which all information necessary to the decision comes together. However, the principle has been honored more in the breach than in practice.

The principle was not widely practiced because (1) many managers received an overabundance of raw data but little of the selected intelligence required for decision making, (2) the data was prepared for the needs of the manager's superior instead of for the manager, and (3) the data was collected for costing and revenue purposes rather than for use by the manager.

MBO places a premium on data prepared under the best principles of enlightened responsibility accounting—the right data, at the right time, at the right place, for the right manager. Now, with in-depth delegation and the proper data, decisions can be made at the lowest possible level, nearest the point of action, at the time the action is taking place.

Accountability. Prior to MBO's requirement for strict accountability by individuals, decisions often were delayed because of what one writer has termed decision drift; that is, the tendency to avoid decision making when it is not clear who should make the decision. Often, the timid manager will purposely delay or ignore making a decision unless he is forced to make it. The undesirable expedient of decision making by committee often results.

By clearly defining who is accountable for what, MBO pinpoints the manager who should make a particular decision. That has definitely lessened procrastination and avoidance of decision making.

Some Pitfalls

MBO has not been a 100 percent success. Many systems have been failures—absolute failures. Others, while not failing completely, have failed to deliver the benefits of which they are capable—failures by degree. Both types of failures have resulted from management's succumbing to the numerous pitfalls that can develop in the system.

The experience of various and diverse organizations over roughly 20 years has singled out a number of reasons for the failure of some organizations to make their mark with MBO. The more prevalent of these pitfalls is discussed later.

MBO Time Shock

The progressive use of MBO within an organization has an attendant time shock for managers. F. D. Barrett, president of Management Concepts, Ltd., describes this shock feature as threefold, coming about when the manager realizes that:

Writing meaningful objectives requires several days, not just a few hours.

The time required to realize the full impact of MBO is not a matter of months but a few years.

A pronounced change takes place in the amount of time the manager spends actually "managing" rather than "doing." Increasingly, doing gives way to managing.[6]

Unfortunately, the impact of this time shock has been too little appreciated by some organizations, and the effectiveness of their MBO approaches has suffered. The impact of this shock—actually it is a necessary period of transition—can neither be ignored nor brought to a forced conclusion. It is as necessary and natural as the progression of a child from adolescence to adulthood. Any attempt to move too rapidly or to fail to gain from the experience arising from the requisite steps will result in an inferior development process.

Future of MBO

Since the application and impact of MBO are yet unfolding, any evaluation must be a dynamic one. However, evidence to date indicates that the effect of MBO has been most dramatic—both on the overall approach to managing and on the many parts of the management process.

Probably its signal benefit has been its insistence on improving organizational effectiveness through improving the effectiveness of the individual manager. This transition has been well summarized by Barrett in his comparison between "Model A" management (pre-MBO) and "Model B" management (post-MBO):

Pre-MBO	*Post-MBO*
Day-to-day managing	Future-focused
Amateur, seat-of-pants	Full-fledged professional
Inward-looking	Outward-looking
Product-oriented	People-oriented
Organization-oriented	Consumer-oriented
Activities-oriented	Results-oriented
Administration of routine	Creation of innovations
Emphasis on "how to"	Emphasis on "what to"
Emphasis on money, machines, materials	Emphasis on people, minds, time

[6] F. D. Barrett, "The MBO Time Trip," *The Business Quarterly,* Autumn 1972, pp. 44–47.

Pre-MBO	*Post-MBO*
Centralized, technocratic, functional control	Decentralized initiative from subordinates
Authoritarian style	Participative style
Directives and supervision	Delegation and reporting
Individualism	Teamwork

The average organization—I dislike the term but am hard pressed to come up with a better description—should expect that this transition will start to take place three to five years after the MBO system is implemented.

MBO and its benefits are too well established, having survived the test of about 20 years of practice, to be considered a passing fancy or a fad. The system has earned its place as part of the permanent management scene. The future will bring the continued use and increased applications of MBO. Real progress remains to be made in several major areas. Managers must become more adept at setting top priorities. As all of an organization's efforts are geared through MBO to meeting top priorities, management's efforts must be directed to insuring that the most desirable priorities are selected. Otherwise, MBO causes an organization to become increasingly efficient at something it should not be doing in the first place.

Having set the optimum priorities, management must increase its competence in planning to achieve the priority objectives. Failure to develop better planning expertise will render it impossible to exploit the full potential of those objectives.

Other areas of the MBO system necessitate continual refinement. For example, even though much progress has been made in relating managerial appraisal to actual contribution, more work remains to be done on this subject. Similarly, additional progress must be made to establish a more direct correlation between a manager's contributions and his rewards. The present tie-in is not direct enough.

In general the effectiveness of MBO will continue to suffer unless an organization's management recognizes that the key word in management by objectives is "management," not "objectives." MBO is a whole new way of life for many organizations. It is a way of managing. Those organizations that embrace the system without recognizing this and without first examining their management philosophy and practice will continue to adopt MBO on a "planned failure" basis. Even worse, they will become easy prey for the increasing number of MBO advocates with a solution who are running around looking for a problem.

The remarkable and continuing growth in numbers of workers in the "knowledge industry" represents another area of high potential payback from MBO. The system has much to commend it for application to these workers. The failure to align their efforts to priorities and fully utilize their talents will constitute a costly oversight for management.

Finally, considerable work needs to be done, and additional experience gained, in applying MBO to the wide variety of organizations in the nonprofit sector. Properly understood and adapted, its promise among nonprofit organizations should be especially bright in light of the magnitude of the job to be done in that sector.

Experience has proved that MBO, by itself, will accomplish nothing but chaos. In the hands of a capable management that is ready for it and knows how to use it, it has much to offer.

DISCUSSION CASE
The Chain of Command

The director of staff development of a public welfare agency was a dedicated believer in organizational planning. Reporting to him was a manager of personnel, who in turn had a supervisor of compensation reporting to him. Every contact made by the supervisor of compensation had to go through the manager of personnel, up to the director of staff development, over to the other division or department head concerned, and then back down through the same chain of command until it reached the original party—the supervisor of compensation. (Several other directors in the organization operated in a similar manner.)

The supervisor of compensation complained that he was getting little done, that his projects were experiencing considerable delay, and that his recommendations and projects often became lost in the confusion.

DISCUSSION POINTS

1. What are the chief weaknesses, if any, in this approach to organization?
2. Discuss the major changes you would recommend to improve organizational effectiveness.

3

Special Considerations

Although there probably is no such thing as a truly unique organization, it would be foolhardy to believe that a management system developed in the private sector can be applied without due regard for the special needs of nonprofit organizations. And, while management is management—regardless of the product, service line, or organization—good management practices must always be applied with due regard to organizational differences. Nonprofit organizations are different in nature from business corporations and the differences must be recognized and accommodated if the benefits of MBO are to be realized.

Needs Determination

The objectives of an organization must be based on the needs it is endeavoring to fulfill or meet. Objectives will suffer when the needs are incorrectly or inadequately determined, or when there is reluctance to pursue every available method for determining them.

Determining the needs a corporation must meet is a fairly straightforward process. Who is the customer? Where is he located? What does he want? What does he consider value? When are his needs met? A corporation that answers these questions incorrectly soon receives negative feedback from its customers. They quit buying!

That is not the case in many nonprofit organizations. Too often, needs are based on *assumptions* of what the "customer" needs and wants. Equally often, there is no effective method of feedback by which the customer can indicate his dissatisfaction or changing needs. Even if he becomes seriously dissatisfied, there is not much he can do about it because he has no alternative source. Many nonprofit services constitute monopolies (for example, government services) because they are the sole source of supply for the given services.

In this connection I am reminded of a recent experience with a research unit in the Air Force. This unit had been spending major sums developing sophisticated avionic systems for combat airplanes. It is undoubtedly difficult to believe that the unit had made no organized, concerted effort to secure feedback from the end users—the combat pilots who actually used the systems. In the absence of this feedback, the research unit in question was running dangerously close to being its own best customer.

Ordering Priorities

Priorities must be determined. To argue otherwise is to support pouring unlimited resources into rapidly expanding and increasingly diverse programs.

The method and basis of determining priorities constitute another major difference. It is infinitely more difficult in most nonprofit organizations. Business concentrates on payback as a chief determinant of priority—where can it realize the greatest benefits for the resources required? Payback does not provide equal guidance in the nonprofit sector. For example, should the health of people take priority over their education? Should defense expenditures take priority over housing for the elderly? Is crime prevention more important than garbage collection? Should paved streets take precedence over aid to dependent mothers?

These questions point out but a few of the perplexing issues that must be faced as priorities are determined. These problems are coupled with the additional complications of elected officials' jockeying for favor with their constituents, of rapidly changing mores and customs, and of confusing and conflicting demands from end users (the public).

The difficulty of ordering priorities has contributed to the sometimes well-founded criticism of nonprofit organizations that they concentrate too much on efficiency without regard to effectiveness. Naturally, it is inadvisable, and often an outright waste of time, to first dwell upon how well something is done (efficiency) before determining what should be done (effectiveness). Thus, in the absence of well-formulated priorities, it is entirely possible to get increasingly more efficient at something that shouldn't be done in the first place. Nonprofit organizations frequently find themselves in this position.

Lack of Management Training

During the preparation of this book, I talked with the administrator of one of the largest nonprofit clinics in the world—one with an annual budget in the high millions. The administrator frankly admitted that his sole exposure to formal management education was a three-day course in basics conducted at a university.

While this experience is not typical of all nonprofit managers (many government agencies, for example, conduct extensive development programs for their managers), it is not uncommon. Managers in the nonprofit sector frequently belong to and actively participate in their professional societies and associations. Far less frequently do they join management societies and associations.

Thus, while these managers are often very well educated in their professions or specialties, a tremendous lag frequently exists in their education in the practice of management. This carries with it the problems usually associated with a specialist in a management (generalist) position.

Lack of Control over Subordinates

Business corporations are well known for organization charts showing the subordinates over whom the manager has control and whom he can direct and discipline for failing to follow directions. This luxury is unavailable to many nonprofit entities.

The large majority of the workers in many nonprofit organizations are nonpaid volunteers who—with almost complete immunity—can tell the organization to go to hell at any time they feel like it. The preponderance of volunteer agencies can be placed in this category; for example, social agencies, blood banks, youth organizations, and community funds.

Volunteers, and for that matter people as a whole, cannot be driven, threatened, or coerced. They must be led. Thus there must be management by challenge and persuasion, and the promotion of maximum interest and participation in worthwhile projects must replace command authority.

Competition for Resources

An excellent example of the common nonprofit approach to planning and budgeting is illustrated by the following case involving a university chancellor.

On July 20, 1974, the chancellor of a large university conducted his annual planning session for the year 1975.

He announced that the total budget for 1975 for all units under his direction would be $10 million allocated individually as follows:

Director of Housing	$ 2 million
Director of Program Development	1 million
Director of Communications Center	3 million
Director of Residence Halls	1 million
Director of Testing Program	2 million
Chancellor's Office	1 million
Total	$10 million

The 1974 budgetary figure represented a reduction of 10 percent from 1973 levels in accordance with a mandate from the governor to increase the productivity of all state activities by a comparable amount.

The chancellor provided the following ground rules to his department heads for their guidance when preparing their plans for 1975:

Emphasis would be on increased productivity.

There would be no lessening of quality standards.

Budgetary allocations would be adhered to strictly, both in total and by individual units.

Final budgets were due on September 1, 1974.

The chancellor concluded the meeting with a pep talk about the satisfaction derived from doing a job well under trying circumstances.

Each of the directors submitted his budget, and the final budget was assembled on September 1. It reflected the following:

Director of Housing	$ 2 million
Director of Program Development	1 million
Director of Communications Center	3 million
Director of Residence Halls	1 million
Director of Testing Program	2 million
Chancellor's Office	1 million
Total	$10 million

The chancellor commended his staff for their planning expertise.

This chancellor's approach is questionable on several grounds and will decrease his effectiveness as well of that of his organization. First, his approach precluded any but a cursory participation on the part of his managers. They parroted back to him what they assumed were predetermined figures and what their boss wanted to hear. Second, he deliberately refused to establish any competition among his managers for the available capital. Those who had been guilty of operating inefficiently in the past were given the same consideration as those who had been breaking their backs and operating in a highly effective manner. Thus emphasis was placed on spending the money made available, not on optimizing results. Third, the chancellor positioned the budget on the wrong end of his so-called planning process. He assigned a cost allowance to each manager without first giving any consideration to priorities and what should be done during the year. Fourth, in the chancellor's approach, control took priority over motivation.

This case illustrates a general tendency in the nonprofit sector to allocate funds to various units and managers without having first established and promoted good, healthy competition for resources, which should always be limited—never unlimited. One research unit of the Department of Defense actually has five committee members on a resource allocation committee who head the units that are vying for the same resources.

It's a management truism that an organization is sick when it fails to establish competition for resources or has more resources than it knows how to utilize. Unlimited resources represent a contradiction to good management.

Role Conflict

Sometimes a serious role conflict exists and must be dealt with. Take, for example, doctors and nurses in a hospital or in the public health service. The more dedicated these people are to their profession, the more difficult it may be for them to adjust to managing with a system like MBO. Unfortunately, these individuals are also managers responsible for multimillion and billion dollar budgets.

The same conflict can develop among other professionals such as ministers, educators, social workers, and volunteers.

Adding to the role conflict is the fact that many managers in these organizations aren't managers because they want to be but because an administrative position is often the only means of promotion, increased compensation, and recognition.

These conflicts must be identified and dealt with. Considerable time and effort often are necessary to reorient these individuals to looking upon themselves as managers first and professionals second.

Motivational Recognition

The types and numbers of motivational rewards and recognition available in business are limited only by the company's coffers, competitive cost levels, and willingness of the corporation's management. This is in marked contrast to many nonprofit organizations. For example, the compensation of federal civil service employees is established by Congress. The manager of a civil service organization cannot vary the compensation policy even though he could motivate better performance among his subordinates if he had the requisite authority.

The long-standing practice of emphasizing seniority rather

than merit when making promotions in government organizations has lessened the impact of this form of recognition. Increasing efforts are being made to measure merit and give it more emphasis. Hopefully, this trend will continue, but the current practice is a problem that must be coped with.

Another prime form of recognition is the granting of authority to managers. Increasing a manager's authority is often equated, in his mind, with receiving a promotion. Here again, many nonprofit organizations can make only limited use of this technique. Authorities, especially in government or quasi-government organizations, are strictly delineated by job, and it is not possible to delegate this authority down the line to subordinates, regardless of how competent and motivated they might be. The director of a welfare department in a large metropolitan area has 27 specific actions for which only he can take action. Even though many of these actions could be handled better at lower levels, he is specifically prohibited from delegating them.

Mandated Actions

Particularly in government organizations, many actions that must be carried out by lower-level managers are mandated from above. This decreases the manager's flexibility in areas such as decision making and in many cases the use of his own discretion.

Often the subject matter of his objectives has been predetermined, as have his resources and target dates for completion. A regional health administrator—who is the top Public Health Service man in each of the ten regions of HEW—may well receive a mandate from higher level that will delineate the subject of his objective, the level of achievement at which the objective must be set, the resources (money and manpower) allotted to him for the objective, and the date by which the objective must be completed. In such cases, he ends up a program administrator or the implementer of someone else's decision making and priority setting.

The voluminous policies and standard operating procedures in a bureaucracy further limit the manager's decision and discretion areas.

In both the above cases, the managers often feel that their voices don't count and aren't listened to. This is often a valid gripe when the organization has not permitted and encouraged lower-level input in top decisions and policies.

Performance Evaluation

At the heart of this subject lies the historical tendency of many nonprofit organizations, especially government-oriented ones, to measure their managers by methods that emphasize effort expended rather than results actually achieved. Many have failed to distinguish between how hard a manager worked and how smart or effectively he worked. Busyness often takes priority over results. Activities become confused with results, and inputs with outputs.

Achievement-oriented managers demand to be measured on accomplishments. They want a factual evaluation as to how well they are performing. They insist on an approach that distinguishes the outstanding contributor from the mediocre or average performer. A manager will not be content for too long with a system that requires him to write concrete objectives and plans and emphasizes positive accomplishments but uses a sloppy measuring stick that fails to identify his contributions.

Short-Term Planning

Frequently, nonprofit organizations concentrate on short-term results without giving adequate attention to the long-term health and growth of the organization and its work. There are many built-in incentives for taking the short-range view.

A politician isn't elected on the basis of the impact his actions may have five, ten, or twenty years from now. His political future depends upon the results he can demonstrate today or in the next few months. A mayor whose term will expire in two years doesn't get particularly excited about taking action to make the next mayor look good.

The attention of generals and admirals, who may be transferred to a new command every two to three years, is directed to today not tomorrow. Even volunteer organizations—in which only the top handful of people are permanent, paid employees—suffer from the often self-serving actions of volunteers who want to look good during the one or two years they may serve. And so it goes.

Additionally, the fairly widespread use of a one-year budget cycle tends to cause short-range focusing. Funds approved for next year may be heavily influenced by the funds approved for this year and by the results that are demonstrated this year.

The direction and guidance that long-term objectives and plans provide to business managers are not commensurately available to many nonprofit managers. Thus nonprofit managers undoubtedly suffer the disadvantage of not being able to realize long-term continuity and results from many of their efforts.

Bureaucracy

Although bureaucracy isn't the exclusive domain of the nonprofit sector, it poses more of a problem there than in the average corporation. These general problems are too well known to dwell upon them here. Suffice it to say that increasingly large organizations, with their attendant red tape, will always face special problems in trying to cope with rapid change and complexity in an environment often fraught with political considerations, decision drift and delay, and needs frequently determined by expediency rather than merit.

Even an overview of some of the special considerations involved when applying MBO to nonprofit organizations might lead the reader to believe that the task is so Herculean as to be unattainable. Such an erroneous impression would miss the whole point of this chapter. Its intent was to briefly highlight some of the more important points that should be addressed. No organization, whether it be profit or nonprofit, is free from its set of problems. One of the prime jobs of any manager is to identify the problems and either eliminate or minimize them.

A major trap that any manager can fall into is believing that his organization or operation is unique and therefore "it can't be applied here." He usually ends up as what is commonly referred to as a "problems-oriented" manager. Whenever a proposal or suggestion is made, his first reaction is to list all the possible problems he can imagine. Often, he never gets around to examining the possible merits or benefits of the proposal. In contrast, the "objectives-oriented" manager first concentrates on the merits or benefits. If they are worthwhile, he then addresses himself to trying to overcome the possible problems.

It is the "objectives-oriented" nonprofit manager who will benefit most from MBO and who will investigate and consider every possible benefit MBO is capable of delivering to his organization. Then he'll formulate ways for adopting the system to his organization with due regard for the special considerations that may exist.

DISCUSSION CASE
The Debatable Productivity-Increase Proposal

The city manager of a large midwestern city received a proposal that, if it could be implemented successfully, would result in an appreciable increase in productivity of most of the personnel through lower costs and greater output. The city manager reviewed the proposal with two groups of his key administrative and managerial personnel.

Group A people state they are already understaffed and overworked. The work flow and procedures would have to be changed. Employees would have to be trained or retrained to handle changed assignments. Morale would suffer. The cost of labor-saving machinery would have to be justified. Employee unrest might cause the Municipal Employees Union to start another organizing attempt. Group A rejects the proposal.

Group B people see the prospect of greater productivity and lower costs. They make a list of the possible problems involved and decide to investigate each one.

DISCUSSION POINTS

1. Are there any basic differences in the approaches of the two management teams? If any, what are they?
2. Describe each group in terms of its probable management characteristics in its day-to-day operating methods.

4

The Objective-Setting Process

The objective-setting process begins with the establishment of the overall objectives and priorities of the organization for the target period under consideration. It then proceeds through each succeeding level of management down the line until objectives have been established at the lowest level to be covered by the system. Usually the lowest level covered is first-line supervision; for example, a section supervisor who has nonsupervisory employees reporting to him.

Differing Approaches

Not all organizations carry out the objective-setting process in the same manner. Many variations are evident as one studies nonprofit organizations. The three following approaches have been tried or recommended to one degree or another by several writers:

1. Hospital A begins its annual objective-setting process by

first stating the overall hospital objectives and then passing them down the line to be used by the lower levels as they set their objectives. (Top down)

2. Hospital B follows the opposite practice by having the process start at the lower levels and then building them up to reach the overall hospital objectives. (Bottom up)

3. Hospital C follows a third approach by endeavoring to establish all objectives at practically the same time through numerous meetings attended by several levels of management and through extensive dialogue. (All at once)

Each approach has serious weaknesses if an attempt is made to follow it as a pure approach.

The Hospital A, or top down, approach will frequently culminate in a situation in which lower-level managers believe the results have been predetermined. They will tend to feed back up the line what they believe the higher levels want to hear. This approach can stifle the participation and dialogue so important to MBO effectiveness.

The weaknesses inherent in the bottom up, or Hospital B, approach center around the differences in managers at different organizational levels. The lower the manager is on the ladder, the more oriented he is to the present. A future-orientation increases as we move up the management ladder. Thus if objectives begin at the bottom, they will be heavily bent to the present, and very often will involve perpetuating the status quo. Another disadvantage is that the lower-level managers will lack any guidance as to what is expected of them.

The Hospital C approach of trying to establish all objectives at once is probably the least effective of all three. Even though it does generate maximum participation, the participation would result in wholesale confusion and chaos except in the extremely small organization with only a handful of managers.

A Better Approach

The subsequent paragraphs illustrate an effective approach commonly followed. It will provide sufficient guidance to the reader so that he may adapt it to the circumstances existing in his own organization.

Two provisions of the definition of MBO that was cited in Chapter 1 serve as the basis for a better approach, one that minimizes the disadvantages of the above three approaches and capitalizes on the advantages: (1) those responsible for directing the organization first establish the overall objectives and priorities, and (2) all managers are required, permitted, and encouraged to contribute their maximum.

Top-Level Objectives

According to this combination approach a "team" is selected to recommend objectives at each level in the organization. For example, let's assume the simplified organization for a hospital shown in Figure 5. The hospital administrator heads the top team, which is indicated by the triangle. The job of this team is to formulate and recommend the broad, all-encompassing objectives of the hospital for the target period. During the three- to five-day meeting that is usually required each year to formulate these objectives, each team member is responsible for helping set the objectives of the hospital as a total entity. He is not concentrating on objectives for his own department; that will come later.

At the conclusion of this meeting, the hospital administrator has a list of possibly six to eight recommended top objectives for the hospital. The following are the kinds of broad objectives that might result from this meeting:

Achieve an average monthly occupancy rate of 80 percent during 1975 without changes in discharging standards.

Figure 5. Simplified hospital organization.

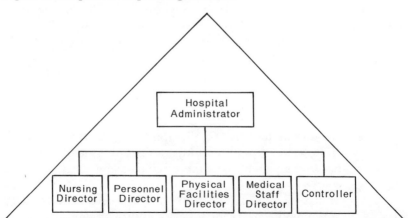

Reduce monthly labor costs to an average of 70 percent of total operating costs by July 1, 1975, and maintain at that level for the remainder of 1975.

Secure by September 1, 1975, accreditation as a nursing school for granting the RN degree.

For the year 1975 reduce total hospital operating costs by 3 percent as compared to 1974 costs.

Next, the administrator (usually with the concurrence of the board of trustees) approves the objectives. This permits objectives to be set at the next level—each of the departments reporting to the administrator, i.e. the directors of nursing, personnel, and physical facilities and the medical staff and the controller.

Lower-Level Objectives

When the overall objectives have been set, each department head and his team recommend departmental objectives. Figure 6, an extension of the previous organization chart, reflects the team

Figure 6. The team of the facilities director.

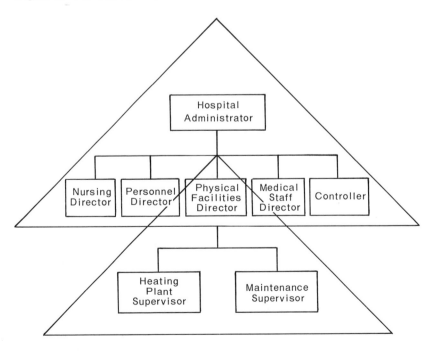

of the physical facilities director. Each of the other directors has a comparable team. The overlapping triangles indicate that the physical facilities director is a member of two teams—the administrator's team and his own.

The job of the physical facilities team is to arrive at a list of recommended objectives for the entire physical facilities department. The overall hospital objectives provide guidance and direction. In effect, the physical facilities team determines what it must accomplish during the target period to insure that its department is helping carry out the overall hospital objectives by determining how they can help achieve the occupancy rate, how they can help reduce labor costs, how they can help secure accreditation as a nursing school, and how they can help reduce total operating costs.

When answered properly, these questions will constitute the subject matter of the objectives this team will recommend for the department as a whole. Once these objectives have been approved, they, plus the overall hospital objectives, serve as the basis for moving the objective-setting process down the line to the next level. The team approach will be repeated again at that level and at all other levels.

Link-Pin Concept

Setting objectives by levels is commonly known as the link-pin concept; it owes its name to the series of overlapping triangles by which it can be portrayed. Figure 7 illustrates the link-pin concept as it might appear for the four levels of management below that of the top director in a state department of public health.

Although this chart shows only the teams emanating from one associate director, it should be noted that each member of Team A has a team, as does each member of Team B. The same is true for each member of Team C.

Objectives at the Lowest Level

As Figure 7 shows, three members of Team D—the section heads—do not have a team because they are the lowest level of management and do not have other managers reporting to them. Normally, the link-pin approach does not contemplate that teams will consist of nonmanagerial employees.

Although the section head probably wouldn't appoint a formal

Figure 7. Link-pin approach to setting multiple-level objectives.

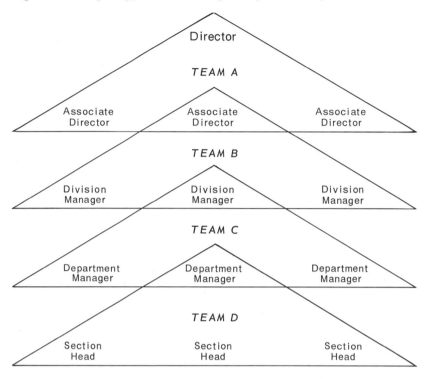

team to help him establish his objectives, he has much to gain by attempting to secure as many recommendations and as much commitment from his people as is practical and possible. They can give him appreciable help in carrying out his objectives, provided they have the interest. Unfortunately, extensive involvement at the employee level often is impossible because of limitations posed by the press of time, unionization of many public employees, and limited ability to delegate authority.

Making Recommendations up the Line

Continuous care must be exercised to prevent the preceding process from ending up in a "top down" approach. Obviously, one of the ways to prevent this is to insure that each team member is given the greatest possible voice in recommending and debating the objectives set at the higher level. For example, the five directors reporting to the hospital administrator should have a major voice in determining the overall hospital objectives. This also requires a willingness on the part of each team member to stand up and be counted, to play an active role rather than a passive one.

There's a second way to encourage the much-needed participation up the line by lower-level managers. Assume, for example, an associate director who is a member of the director's team. The associate director knows that on a certain date he must participate with all other associate directors in helping establish the overall objectives for the organization. Well in advance of the meeting, if he's smart, he'll take advantage of every possible opportunity to secure the recommendations and comments of each of the managers below him. This can be accomplished by a combination of meetings, telephone calls, face-to-face contact, and written communications. Thus he enters the team meeting armed with not only his own thinking and recommendations but also that of his subordinate managers.

DISCUSSION CASE
The XYZ Volunteer Organization

You have been retained as an MBO consultant to XYZ, a volunteer organization.

XYZ's mission is to teach young men and women of high school age the economics and operation of the private enterprise system by providing them with the opportunity to organize and operate a "mini-business" for a few hours each week after school. At the beginning of each school year, XYZ's regional directors solicit business companies to sponsor a group of high school students. The students who have been recruited are assigned to a sponsoring company. This group organizes a "company," which elects its own officers and managers, determines what product it will produce and market and what its sales and pricing policy will be, does its own purchasing and production, and generally manages and operates the business as if it were a real company. A manager of the sponsoring company acts as an adviser, but lets the young men and women make their own decisions and solve the many problems that develop. Products of these "mini-businesses" range from first-aid kits to baby furniture and toys. The "company" is considered successful if it has earned a profit at the end of the year.

XYZ is headed by a nonpaid board of directors usually consisting of practicing businessmen who provide overall advice and counsel. Although one of them serves as president, the full-time executive direction of the organization is the responsibility of the executive director. He is a paid, full-time professional.

The company has five regions throughout the United States, each headed by a full-time regional director who reports to the executive director. The major responsibilities of regional directors are to direct and administer XYZ's programs in the region, recruit sponsor companies and high school students for participation in the program, and act as an overall adviser to sponsoring companies and the participating students as they operate their companies.

XYZ depends almost exclusively upon voluntary contributions for its resources. Expenses consist primarily of salary and administrative costs of operating the national and regional offices. During the past several years, the number of sponsoring companies and students has continued to increase at a modest rate. Contributions have been sufficient to sustain the growth. XYZ's management is concerned about the increasing competition from the many other organizations for corporate contributions and support. It anticipates that companies will become increasingly critical of the uses to which its contributions are put. It believes the adoption of management by objectives will help it earn, and be able to demonstrate, a high return on each dollar it receives in contributions. It presently has no objectives or goals with the exception of endeavoring to be as effective as possible with the contributions it receives.

DISCUSSION POINTS

1. Discuss the relationship the executive director should endeavor to establish with his board of directors.
2. Highlight the primary roles of the board and the executive director (and his staff) in implementing and operating under MBO.
3. What major problems are likely to develop if the proper relationship is not established?

5

Writing
Meaningful Objectives

As already stated, the purpose of MBO is not to have managers arrive at a list of objectives. The purpose of MBO is to help managers achieve more significant results. While this may sound like a play on words, the distinction is crucial to successful MBO practice.

A common failure of managers when writing their objectives is to start out writing the objective itself. The usual result of such an exercise is a list of rather sterile objectives that have little value and meaning; they don't become a living, viable means of helping the manager manage his job. This failure frequently results from emphasizing the wrong word in the term "management by objectives." The key word is the word "management." It is not the word "objectives," regardless of their importance to the system.

Objectives are part of the management system; they aren't the system itself. Without an effective management system in which objectives are properly written and which facilitates translating them into practice, objectives are worthless.

The Sequence of Objective Setting

Meaningful objectives will result only if the manager has completed the necessary steps or preparatory work leading up to the point at which the actual writing of objectives takes place. Figure 8 illustrates the steps in the objective-setting process. This flow chart dramatically illustrates that objectives are written at Step 7, not Step 1. The first six steps help the manager prepare to write meaningful objectives. Steps 8 through 13, the steps following the writing of objectives, insure that the objectives are translated into action—that they become a way of life and not just a list of objectives.

There are good reasons for emphasizing the preceding paragraphs. No matter how we might try to avoid the connotation, "objectives" receive so much attention that many managers come to believe that they are the system and not part of it. Objectives are invariably meaningless unless they operate within a system of managing.

Each of the steps shown in Figure 8 is illustrated in actual practice in Chapter 15, the case history of MBO in a church organization. To prevent repetition and save the reader's time, they are not repeated here. He may want to read Chapter 15 before finishing the rest of this chapter, which discusses the writing of objectives at Step 7.

What Is an Objective?

Before beginning Step 7, let's define what an objective is. An objective is a specific description of an *end result* to be achieved. It should tell *what* (the end result), *when* (a target date or a target period), and *who* (who is accountable for the objective).

Writing the Objective

Assuming that the preliminary work has been satisfactorily completed, the manager is now ready to formulate his objectives. Objectives should meet several criteria or tests.

Priorities. Management consists in the continual addressing of efforts to accomplishing the priorities of the organization. In line with this, objectives normally involve the high-priority portions of

Figure 8. The objective-setting process.

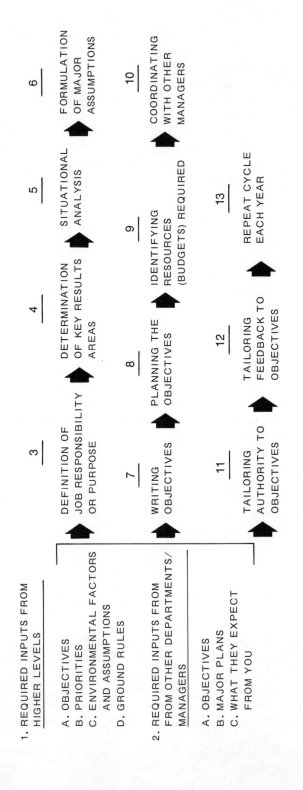

a manager's job. Usually, objectives are not set for the routine maintenance, or "housekeeping," chores, which are a part of every managerial job. Covering the routine aspects would frequently lead to a manager's having a long laundry list of objectives in which the important and the routine become combined and confused.

Some organizations make an exception to the principle that objectives should cover only priority matters. For example, a manager might be required to temporarily have as the subject of an objective a routine matter that has become so fouled up that it is hampering operations. The problem is covered by an objective until he corrects the problem. Then it reverts back to the routine category. This is an excellent method of keeping the spotlight on trouble areas.

Another exception comes into play with certain lower-level management jobs; for example, a program administrator in a government agency. Frequently, the bulk of his job requires him to direct several programs at once. In this case, "routine" and "priority" may mean about the same thing. His job consists primarily in the day-to-day administering of ongoing programs.

Sometimes these routine objectives are basic to the job. How should they be handled? The most appropriate method for evaluating whether an individual has achieved them is to insure that he is aware of the objectives. The manager must tell the subordinate, early in the relationship, what the activities of the job are and what the desired level of performance is. Evaluation should only follow a previous discussion of criteria.

At the same time that the criteria are being made specific, acceptable tolerance limits should be developed. Measurement of the routine should be a major part of the objective-setting process, but it is of most concern when performance falls outside acceptable levels. Essentially, it is proposed that minimum performance levels be set for routine activities. Evaluation of routine goals should be by exception, or when these standards are not met.

Naturally, the ability to manage by exception demands good plans or clear standards from which exceptions can be specified in advance. Odiorne cites the following example:

> The paymaster, for example, may report that his routine duties cluster around getting the weekly payroll out every Friday. It is agreed that the measure of exception will be zero—in other words, the boss should expect no exceptions to the diligent performance of this rou-

tine duty. Thus, the failure any week to produce the payroll on Friday will be considered an exception that calls for explanation by the subordinate. If the cause were reasonably under his control or could have been averted by extra care or effort, the absence of the payroll will be considered a failure on the part of the subordinate.[1]

Should be specific. The first requirement is that the objective be specific and measurable to the maximum extent possible. The first draft of objectives for the commander of an air defense interceptor squadron read as follows: "To become airborne and engage all unidentified aircraft in the shortest possible time."

This vague, general statement of intent is incapable of being measured. Additionally, it is so vague that it provides little guidance to the commander or his subordinates and because the desired result is not clear, there is no way the commander and his people can plan for achieving it. Obviously, the relative words "shortest possible" must be defined.

Words such as "shortest possible" are considered weasel words. Other examples of weasel words are: *reasonable, justifiable, maximum, allowable, highest, lowest,* and *desirable.* All these are relative terms that convey different meanings to different people. The presence of a weasel word will invariably destroy the effectiveness of an objective; the word should be eliminated and replaced by a specific definition of what is intended.

The objective of the squadron commander is made more specific and measurable by rewording it to read: "By August 1, 1975, all alert aircraft to be airborne within five minutes of receiving alert, with all systems operational for engaging assigned targets."

Results versus activities. The definition of an objective indicated that it is a specific statement of an *end result.* Thus an objective should address itself to results, not activities in which one may engage to achieve the result.

An example of an activity is illustrated by the following objective submitted by a chief of a training section: "Conduct six training sessions for OHSA (Occupational Health and Safety Act) field inspectors."

The question that must be raised here is: "Why?" What is the purpose of the training? What is it intended to accomplish? What is the end result being sought? This objective is better expressed as follows: "Train six OHSA field inspectors by June 1, 1975, so

[1] George S. Odiorne, *Management By Objectives* (New York: Pitman, 1964), p. 104.

they meet the standards for completing field inspections in accordance with the Act."

Should be realistic and attainable. Objectives should be realistic and attainable at all times. It is self-defeating to set unrealistic objectives or to refuse to revise them if subsequent events demonstrate that the objectives are based on false assumptions or if insurmountable problems are encountered.

Objectives, and plans to achieve them, should never be considered as having been carved in stone. Such a false notion precludes their being used as a living, viable means of managing.

Should contain "stretch." MBO contemplates continual improvement on the part of managers. Therefore, objectives should be set at a level of difficulty and achievement that requires managers to exert more than normal effort or a business-as-usual approach. There is no easy formula for determining how much stretch an objective should require. Essentially, the determination of stretch must be based on the superior's evaluation of the subordinate's objectives in light of the probable circumstances that will exist during the target period. To the extent the information can be secured, the following will serve as useful guides—but only guides—in determining stretch:

Superior's observation and knowledge of subordinate's capability, drive, motivation, and so on.

Subordinate's past record.

Subordinate's recommendations and comments as to how much stretch he has included.

Performance levels of other managers on the same or similar jobs in the organization.

Subordinate's performance on similar jobs in other organizations.

External requirements; for example, legal requirements may establish the minimum level at which the manager must perform.

Demands of the situation; for example, user or client demands, higher-level demands, and demands of other departments may establish minimum performance levels.

Should match experience and capability. One of the major virtues of MBO is that it can serve as a means of management development. However, the full realization of this benefit requires matching the complexity and difficulty of objectives to the experience and capability of the manager. Set too high, the objectives can lead to frustration and thwarting of development. Set too low, they can demotivate the manager. Particular care in this regard must be exercised when working with the newer, less experienced manager.

Should be consistent with responsibility and authority. All objectives should cover matters for which the manager is organizationally responsible, and he must have the necessary authority to carry out the objectives. The following is an example of the type of objective frequently recommended by managers who are new to the MBO system. This objective was recommended by the personnel manager of a medium-size hospital: "Lower the average monthly absentee rate to 8 percent by April 30, 1975."

This objective is not consistent with his responsibility or authority and if it is approved, his chances of achieving it are remote. His responsibility doesn't include all the components involved in controlling absenteeism, and his authority is not sufficiently broad for him to be able to reduce or control absenteeism. Much of the responsibility for controlling absenteeism rests with the individual line managers to whom the employees report.

Objectives should be updated. Normally, objectives should change from one target period to the next. This helps to prevent the perpetuation of obsolete programs and helps to insure that managers continue to address their efforts to constantly changing priorities and needs. Managers should be required to observe strict standards of justification when they propose to carry over a particular objective from one target period to the next.

Number of objectives. Obviously, there is no set number of objectives for all managers. However, if the commonly accepted principle is followed that objectives should cover only the highest-priority matters for the target period, then setting somewhere around five to seven major objectives is probably a good rule of thumb for most managers. This number usually increases in the case of specialists who deal primarily in programs and specific projects; for example, a program administrator in many government departments, compared to other managers whose objectives are broader and all-encompassing, such as a department head.

Vertical and horizontal compatibility. Objectives are not an end in themselves, nor are they written exclusively for the manager and his department. Thus all objectives written in any unit of the department must be compatible with and help carry out the higher-level objectives (vertical compatibility). They must also be supportive of the objectives of other departments and units (horizontal compatibility). Double checking all objectives for this dual compatibility helps insure that the department is carrying out its required role and that the necessary coordination and communications with other units have been effected.

Wording of objectives. Contrary to the counsel of some writers, there is no set wording or format that will cover the multiplicity of objectives emanating from the many units of an organization. Rather than trying to follow a set format, managers should devote primary emphasis to having the objective—regardless of the wording used—meet the criteria discussed in these paragraphs.

Obviously, the better the job a manager does in the objective-writing stage, the better off he will be as he completes the post-objective-setting stage and proceeds to translate his objectives into practice. Specific, measurable objectives, which are clearly understood by all concerned, are the basis for tailoring meaningful evaluation, feedback, and monitoring techniques to help the manager manage better.

DISCUSSION CASE
Analyzing and Evaluating Objectives

Here are some first-draft objectives that have been recommended by a number of managers in various types of organizations.

DISCUSSION POINTS

Evaluate and discuss the effectiveness of each objective in light of the commonly accepted criteria for making objectives effective.

Director, division of criminal investigation: Establish and implement by July 1, 1975, a public relations campaign for the division of criminal investigation to portray to the general public the division's activities in assisting and/or supplementing local law enforcement.

Consultant, office of administration: As consultant to the commissioner of administration, develop clearly defined lines of responsibility accountability and authority for each of the division directors by November 1, 1975.

Management analyst: Develop and implement improved contract review and approval procedures so that by the end of fiscal year 1975 the mean time for the review/approval cycle will be reduced to 30 days and all contracts approval will conform with state policies and support state-approved plans.

Senior management analyst: Complete the implementation of 109 of the recommendations resulting from XYZ Program by the end of the 1975–1976 fiscal year.

Consultant to community services director: Establish program priorities and funding criteria (consistent with federal revenue-sharing guidelines and state code) with the Township Youth Committee by March 1, 1975.

Senior management analyst: Conduct preliminary review of State A's MBO system by October 5, 1974, with recommendations on the feasibility of applying compatible MBO systems to our MBO approach to be presented to the MBO task force by October 20, 1974.

Chief executive officer: Increase institutional mission awareness by all managers by having them attend seminar on institutional mission during year 1975.

Manager, maintenance and housekeeping: Improve maintenance to get 80 percent customer satisfaction.

Mayor: Have city council pass a tax stabilization policy by January 1, 1976.

Executive director of children's medical and dental clinic: Improve communication between departments to enable employees (department heads) to enjoy a free exchange of ideas, share concerns, and eliminate problems that cross departmental lines. Target date: one month.

Multiservice center director: Enhance employee productivity by a 5 percent increase in number of casework services rendered by July 1, 1976.

Department administrator: Initiate a hot meal program to improve the health of the elderly in the neighborhood by serving 100 meals daily by July 1975.

Contracting officer: Inventory and prepare accounting records for all contractor-installed equipment not later than six months after activation of new hospital.

Administrative office, community service center: Generate $90,000 foundation funding commitment by March 1975 for a three-year Spanish-speaking community service center.

Warning officer: Develop warning plans for four additional counties by July 1, 1975.

Assistant director: Improve staffing ratio from the present 1:7 to 1:8 by June 30, 1975.

Manpower and Organization Division, Defense Nuclear Agency: Reduce the fiscal year 1975 end strength authorization of the Defense Nuclear Agency by 12 percent (215 spaces); reductions programmed at the rate of 150 spaces by June 30, 1975; 65 remaining spaces by June 30, 1976.

Maintenance manager: For the purpose of establishing standards, work schedules, and costs, design a worksheet that would quickly identify all rooms, square feet of floors, walks, ceilings, windows, and the type of material for all buildings by January 1, 1976.

Director, personnel management division: Reduce the turnover rate to less than the agency rate (approximately 17 percent) within one year.

Regional administrator: By June 30, 1975, reduce by one month the mean length of time it takes to process (from receipt of formal request to procurement or assignment of space) an agency's request for space.

Executive director, social services: Develop within one year an evaluation process to determine the impact of program on participants to add substance and validity to program planning.

Management analyst: Present recommendations of feasibility to influence top division administrators to begin implementation of MBO by July 1, 1975.

Village (city) manager: Devise new methods to monitor and react to proposed state legislation during the next legislative year that affects cities and village governments and departments.

Director of education: Twenty hours of in-service training per employee per quarter in effective training-needs analysis.

Administrative resident: Act as department head in one professional and one service department for at least two months each within next six months.

President of administrative services: Through education, obtain top-level management acceptance of MBO system within six months.

Training director: Increase by 10 percent from base measurement the use of indirect teaching behaviors in a designated teaching assignment.

Program director, alcoholism treatment center: Increase average daily census from 80 percent to 90 percent of capacity.

Assistant director of education and training: Implement a

self-instructional systems approach to nursing assistant training by December 1975.

Chief of interpretation: Improve visitor information services by increasing operations at two information stations by a total of 38 man-days in June, July, and August 1975.

Executive director of mental health center: Have 450 non-duplicated clients use services of the mental health center during target period of one year.

Chief of maintenance: Cut down on lost time, personnel accidents, and damage to government equipment.

Executive director of mental health center: Develop more efficient staff utilization by decreasing nondirect service staff hours by 10 percent as reported by the management information system.

Executive director, camp school: By December 31, 1976, hire and train ten live-in camp counselors with at least six remaining and maintaining their camp by December 31, 1976.

Executive director: Following the approval of the NIMH child grant to be initiated September 1, 1974, the executive director will commence personnel recruitment activities for the final selection of eight clinical and two administrative support personnel by October 15, 1974, to comprise the consultation–education unit of the program. Following the selection of personnel by October 15, 1974, the executive director will constitute three task forces in the three highest predetermined priority areas for program development to achieve a finalized organizational decision; namely, organizational development, staff development, interdisciplinary training. Task forces constituted October 15 and reports presented to total staff November 1, 7, 14 respectively.

Maintenance manager: (1) Upgrade the level of customer satisfaction by 10 percent. (2) Reduce the amount of building damage by 10 percent. (3) Create a system of feedback to residents on accomplishments. (4) Develop a training program for all levels of employees. (5) Increase quality of housekeeping. (6) Develop a plan for knowing the stage of completion and cost of physical plant work orders. (7) Develop a worksheet to show the square footage of all rooms, floors, walks, and windows in each building.

6

Monitoring
and Controlling

The primary purpose of MBO, as noted earlier, is not to write objectives but to provide managers with a living, viable means of realizing a higher level of results. Thus there is absolutely no reason for writing objectives unless these objectives are translated into continuing action during the target period.

The two primary means to bring objectives to life are the carrying out of the step-by-step action plans for achieving the objectives and the control and monitoring phase, which must keep managers continuously informed as to how well their objectives and plans are being achieved.

Why Control?

Feedback on performance is an absolute requirement for two vitally important reasons. The first has to do with the requirements of an achievement-oriented manager. The second purpose of feedback is to permit the manager to stay on target by making interim decisions and revisions during the target period.

Achievement orientation. A large body of experience and knowledge has proved the soundness of the following premises:

1. The more achievement-oriented a manager is, the more he demands feedback on his performance. He wants to know how well he's doing at all times.

2. The more achievement-oriented a manager is, the less tolerant he is of paperwork, unnecessary routines, and raw data. He wants a minimum amount of data—data that is organized so as to constitute "intelligence" on which he can base his decisions and take action.

Interim decisions and revisions. Once objectives and plans have been approved, they can't just be filed away and forgotten. They must be used as a guide to required action during the target period. Thus the manager must always know how well or how poorly he's performing. He must know at the earliest possible time when his plans aren't working out. Otherwise, he can't take corrective action and make the revisions that are sometimes necessary to keep his objectives and plans realistic at all times. In the absence of timely, meaningful feedback, he runs a strong chance of having his operation get out of control and his objectives and plans become obsolete.

Types of Feedback

The two types of feedback we shall emphasize are:

1. The continuous, day-to-day feedback the manager needs to track progress on his objectives and plans. This may be called operational feedback. It is tailored for, and used primarily by, the manager himself.

2. Periodic feedback, generally in the form of performance appraisal, or evaluation, by the manager's boss. Both the manager and his boss are very much involved in this form of feedback.

This chapter will concern itself with day-to-day operational feedback. The next chapter will address itself to performance appraisal, or evaluation.

Traditional Weaknesses

"Control" has often been considered a dirty word. Many times it was prepared by accountants with a "looking backward" orientation. Top management overemphasized mistakes instead of providing its line managers with future-oriented information on which positive action could be taken. As a natural result, feedback often became associated with gigging or auditing managers.

In some companies the information was collected primarily for revenue or costing purposes without regard to the needs of the individual managers who might be involved in the actions that generated the revenue or created the costs. Sometimes the information was prepared for the wrong person—often not for the manager on the firing line but for his supervisor.

In the past, attempts were made to provide specific feedback on general matters. This is a contradictory situation because control implies specificity. For example, in the absence of specific objectives and plans, the manager's responsibility was very general and nebulous. Applying specific controls became very difficult at best. Overcontrol frequently resulted.

Traditional feedback also has been plagued by an overabundance of the wrong type of information, which the hapless manager must plow through in attempting to locate the one or two nuggets of information he really needs. This problem has compounded with the advent of the computer. Many organizations continue to operate with fourth-generation hardware and first-generation computer personnel.

Emphasizing the Positive

The exacting requirements for feedback will be met only if those responsible will emphasize the positive—if they'll stop looking backward on a gigging, auditing basis and switch their focus to the future. Future-oriented feedback helps keep the manager out of trouble in the first place by spotting trouble for him as quickly as possible. Also, it treats feedback as a decision-making tool rather than as a hanging device for mistakes. It must emphasize helping the manager "improve" and not be based on making him "prove it."

Emphasizing the Individual

Much of the success of MBO lies in the increased motivation and commitment that results from putting each manager "in business for himself." Self-supervision, self-management, and self-

control are the keys to establishing this much-sought entrepre-
neurial relationship. And all of them act in concert.

Self-supervision means that once the manager and his boss
have agreed upon the objectives to be achieved, the subordinate
should be fairly free to supervise himself with only minimal (but
effective) control from above. Self-management means that once
the two parties agree to the resources that have been allocated
(budget), the manager should be free to manage those resources.

Naturally, if the emphasis is on self-supervision and
management, then commensurate emphasis must be placed on
self-control. The manager must be in a position to properly control
those matters he is supervising and managing. He cannot supervise and manage unless he can also control at his level.

Thus controls must be designed and tailored primarily for the
manager who is accountable for achieving the objectives—not for
his boss. This chapter will show the step-by-step tailoring of feedback to individual objectives.

The difference between feedback that has not been tailored to
the firing-line manager and that which has been can be illustrated
by comparing two feedback loops—one traditional and one tailored—showing how a variance is corrected under both systems.

Figure 9 illustrates how a variance is commonly corrected
under traditional feedback. It has eight steps. Obviously, the primary weakness shown in Figure 9 is that the feedback goes to
the manager's superior.

Figure 10 illustrates the correction of a variance under tailored feedback. There are only three steps. In this illustration, the
feedback has been tailored to the objectives of the firing-line manager. The corrective action is made by the person nearest the
scene of the action. Also, the time lag is avoided because the manager does not have to wait for his boss to direct that corrective action be taken.

Components of Operational Feedback

Under an MBO system there are five major areas that serve as
the major sources of control for the manager. These are the very
minimum points on which he must insure that controls have been
established and for which he must receive meaningful feedback
information. They are:

Figure 9. Correcting a variance under traditional feedback.

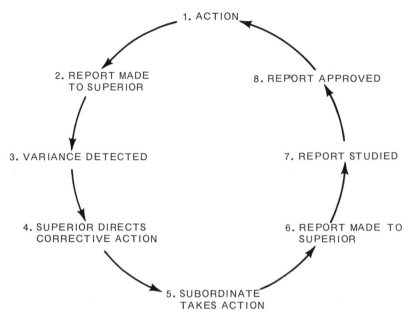

Figure 10. Correcting a variance under decentralized feedback.

1. Control of assumptions.
2. Control of objectives—the priority parts of the job.
3. Control of plans.
4. Control of resources.
5. Control of routine activities.

Control of Assumptions

This is one of the more commonly neglected control points. As noted earlier, it is not possible to establish objectives—which always cover a future period—without basing them on major assumptions that are formulated during the objective-setting process. The assumptions on which the objectives and plans are based must be clearly stated and tracked continuously during the target period to determine if they are valid.

To illustrate use of assumptions for the purposes of control, let's say that a manager's objectives are based on eight assumptions, which he has formulated. Let's further assume that he is a Department of Defense manager who must buy large amounts of expensive electronic equipment. One of his eight assumptions reads as follows: "It is assumed that inflation will continue at the rate of 10 percent during 1975."

Naturally, wherever costs have entered his 1975 objectives, he has predicated them on this assumption about inflation. We'll now assume his objectives have been approved and that the target year 1975 has started to unfold. On March 1 of 1975 he examines the actual rate of inflation and learns that it is 15 percent as opposed to the 10 percent he assumed. This immediately warns the manager that his objectives are based on an assumption that is not coming true. It also tells him that a new assumption is called for and that he must formulate a new assumed rate of inflation. Even more importantly, it tells him that he must revise one or more of the following: his objectives, his plans to achieve them, or his resource allocation. This is the first method by which the manager keeps his objectives and plans updated and realistic at all times.

It should be noted that assumptions can act as the early warning system described above only if all assumptions have been clearly stated, have been recorded, and are constantly monitored.

Control of Objectives

Objectives must be measurable to the maximum extent possible; otherwise control becomes practically impossible. Consider for example an objective that reads: "Make a substantial increase in the efficiency of my department by September 1, 1975."

The use of the highly subjective word "substantial"—frequently referred to as a weasel word—makes it impossible to measure performance on the objective and thus to control that performance. Additionally, it is not possible to lay out plans to achieve the objective because no two people would agree as to what end result is being sought.

Now compare this with the following well-worded objective for the regional manager of a volunteer agency concerned with training high school students in the principles of operating a business: "Achieve 12 percent student penetration in the organization's programs during the 1975 program year."

MBO requires that meaningful feedback be tailored to the individual objectives of the manager. Here is a five-step method for tailoring the feedback to the objective of the regional manager:

Step 1. Statement of the objective: Achieve 12 percent student penetration in organization's programs during 1975 program year.

Step 2. Definition of the measure to be used for monitoring performance: Total number of young people ages 15 to 18 inclusive in all four counties divided into number participating for at least three-quarters of school year.

Step 3. How often feedback will be provided (based primarily on how often the manager is in a position to take remedial action): Monthly.

Step 4. Determination, on a need-to-know basis, of who should get copies of the report: Regional manager, area director, executive vice-president–secretary.

Step 5. Description of the form in which the report will be presented (the simpler, the better): Special-purpose report.

The results of this process assure the manager that he is receiving meaningful feedback designed primarily for his use. The same data may be used for other purposes, such as costing and reports for higher-level managers, but the primary emphasis is on the manager's needs.

Control of Plans

The step-by-step plans by which the manager has decided to achieve his objective serve as another excellent means of control for him. However, they will serve this purpose only if they are prepared in enough detail; that is, they are broken down into several distinct action steps and a timetable for completion of each step has been agreed to. For example, the plan that supports the following objective of a high school principal is worthless when it comes to establishing controls.

Objective	*Plans*
By December 31, 1975, lower the high school dropout rate among seniors by 10 percent over the year 1974.	Analyze the reasons for dropouts during the past three years and prepare and implement methods of reducing the rate.

This principal didn't construct enough detailed steps and failed to establish interim target dates or a timetable for use during the year. He won't know until the target period is over—when there's no time left for corrective action—whether he's achieved his objective. Interim measuring, correcting, and revising during the target period have become impossible.

Figure 11 illustrates how the same objective was planned out by action steps and dates to permit the interim control to be established.

Control of Resources

The function and use of budgets and budgetary control are too well known to belabor. We should note, however, that budgets should be viewed as the allocation of resources to objectives; in other words, the budget is tailored to the objectives and plans. Also, budget reporting must follow good principles of responsibility accounting, with all status and variance reports going primarily to the manager responsible for the objectives and plans.

Figure 11. Plans to achieve objectives.

MANAGER RESPONSIBLE:	Director of Parent Services
OBJECTIVE #4:	During the calendar year 1975, increase to 6.03 percent the number of people reunited with their children.
MEASURE:	Number of parents reunited, divided by all parents with high potential for being reunited.

Major Action Steps	January-December											
	J	F	M	A	M	J	J	A	S	O	N	D
1. Define criteria for determining eligibility for being reunited (high potential).	x											
2. Select those eligible for being reunited.		x										
3. Develop pilot program.			x									
4. Implement pilot program for x percent of those who are eligible.				x								
5. Evaluate results of pilot program.						x						
6. Revise program as necessary on the basis of the evaluation.						x						
7. Implement revised program for y percent of those eligible.							x					
8. Evaluate results of revised program.										x		
9. Determine future action.												x

Control of Routine Activities

Normally, objectives cover only the more important or priority parts of the job during the target period. As indicated earlier, controls are then established to monitor performance on these priority objectives.

This leaves for consideration the control and monitoring of the routine parts of the job, which aren't covered by objectives. Thus an important policy decision at this point becomes determining how much control is desirable or necessary over this routine. Practice varies widely. Some organizations insist upon complete control of objectives and leave control of the routine to the individual manager. Others demand that both priority and routine activities be controlled rather tightly.

One practical way—but one that must be used with discretion lest violence be done to effective delegation—is to reduce the priority actions to objectives, as has been recommended in this book, and then tailor controls to them. Next, the routine parts of the job are embodied in "standards of performance."

The basic difference between "objectives" and "standards of performance" in this context is that objectives are self-liquidating; that is, they usually end when the target period is reached, while standards of performance may continue from one target period to the next without being changed. Examples of standards of performance are:

> Performance is satisfactory when payroll checks are distributed on time 51 out of 52 weeks.

> Performance is satisfactory when the average monthly absentee rate does not exceed x percent.

> Performance is satisfactory when 99 percent of the grievances with the Municipal Employees Union are processed within the time limits specified in the contract.

Once these standards of performance have been established, they are controlled by the exception principle.

Corrective Action and Revisions

It should be obvious that the feedback report itself is not the end being sought. What is being sought is the action that the report should activate—corrective action to stay on target or necessary revisions to objectives, plans, or budgets so that they are always realistic and being followed.

We should note that a competent MBO manager doesn't take revisions lightly, especially downward revisions from previously established levels. Before ever requesting a downward adjustment in his objectives, he first considers leaving the objective at the same level and first exploring every possible alternative for making up for whatever unfavorable variance may have occurred. In fact the two hallmarks of a competent MBO manager are, first, a manager who is willing to devote the time and effort necessary to establish realistic objectives in the first place and, second, to be completely unwilling to lower the objective unless he has first pursued every possible way of meeting it.

DISCUSSION CASE
Control of Absenteeism

The director of a Department of Defense unit was briefing his managers about some of the problems facing the unit. Among other problems, he was concerned about the high costs resulting from the absentee rate for clerical workers, which has been averaging about 12 percent in Department A. Both the department manager and the personnel manager shared the director's concern and the problems resulting from hiring and training temporary employees, lower productivity of the temporary replacements, work disruptions, payments made to absentees, and other related costs and inconveniences.

All three managers agreed that the department head and the personnel manager should work together during the coming year to reduce the problems and costs of absenteeism. The director stated that all possible efforts should be devoted to reducing the average monthly rate to 8 percent by the end of the next eight months. Another meeting would be held eight months later to review results.

The follow-up meeting was held as scheduled. A heated debate ensued. The director chewed out both the department and the personnel manager because the absentee rate had decreased to only 11 percent. In turn, the department head criticized the personnel manager for poor record keeping and for not investigating questionable sicknesses. The personnel manager blamed the director for handing out an unreasonable assignment and the department head for failing to take proper disciplinary action against the offenders. The meeting ended when the director terminated the shouting match and indicated he would call another meeting when tempers, including his own, had cooled off.

DISCUSSION POINTS

1. What might you have done differently eight months earlier to promote more effective delegation and control of the delegated accountability?
2. Prior to the next meeting you want to plan for making delegation more effective. You continue to believe that absenteeism is a major problem and want the personnel manager and the department head to emphasize reducing it. Briefly outline your plan.

7

Performance Evaluation

Because of the overabundance of the written and spoken word on the subject of performance evaluation, it will be time well spent to devote a few words to reexamining why we evaluate the performance of managers in the first place. Clearly, there appear to be four solid reasons for measuring managers:

1. As a means for motivating the achievement-oriented manager;
2. As the basis for rewards (salary increases, incentive compensation, service awards, time off, and promotions);
3. As the basis for discipline (static job status, demotion, discharge);
4. As a guide for individualized training and development requirements.

Even a casual review of the above reasons will reveal that they go straight to the heart of what makes a successful management group. They are the make-or-break aspects of an organization's progress.

Assuming the importance of these matters has been correctly gauged—and I suggest that most top managers would agree with the ranking—why should there be so much nonsense and wasted effort connected with the evaluation process?

Defects in the Evaluation Process

First, much of the difficulty results from the traditional approach to have all of us attempt to qualify ourselves as pseudo-psychologists and sociologists when we evaluate our subordinates. Instead of insisting that we evaluate our subordinate managers on the basis of the concrete results they achieve (or fail to achieve) the personality-oriented traditionalists would have us rate our people on such nebulous—and almost irrelevant—factors as how well they get along with their people and the status of their health. While trite, the way a person parts his hair probably continues to be a key evaluation factor in more organizations than we would care to admit.

Another defect in the process is that we often attempt to measure performance without first determining how and what we are measuring; that is, we try to measure without having first established a standard against which the measuring will take place. Expressed another way, if we are to measure a manager's effectiveness, we must first decide and agree on some definition of "effectiveness."

For example, one of the factors most commonly found on managerial appraisal forms is: "Degree to which the manager is cost-conscious." There is no way in the world a manager could be evaluated on this factor unless his superior had first determined: that for the manager's particular job, for the particular evaluation period, under the particular circumstances that prevailed, the spending of x amount of money was an acceptable standard for a cost-conscious manager.

A third obstacle to effective evaluation is trying to compensate for the inadequacies of the evaluation process by making it replete with long, complicated recording forms and high-sounding words and requiring an excessive amount of time and effort for the superior to rate the subordinate. The watchword of this school would appear to be: Make it big, pretentious, and time-consuming and it will at least sound effective.

Another problem, and this one should be labeled "Myth

Number 4," is the much advocated, but meaningless theory that the evaluation process should be used solely for development purposes and never, but never, should rewards such as salary increases be connected with the process. Who do we think we're kidding? When we evaluate a manager and discuss his evaluation with him, it is patently ridiculous and actually dangerous to purposely ignore the question always uppermost in his mind; namely, "Yeah! I hear you boss, but what does it mean to my paycheck?"

As managers we make the biggest mistake when we base the future of both the organization and its managers on any evaluation process that isn't the best and most accurate we can make it. When we use an inadequate measuring device, chances are we are rewarding the undeserving, failing to recognize the real performers, and as a result not giving our organizations the value to which they are entitled from our stewardship.

Repairing the Defects

Fortunately, there's nothing magic or complicated about correcting the problems. Basically, we need to adopt an approach to evaluating managers that is based on:

1. Acceptance that managers must be measured on the results they actually achieve, not on what they say they will do, not on the amount of time and effort they expend, and certainly not on their ability to win a popularity contest.
2. Establishment of standards (key results and objectives) against which performance will be measured.
3. Actual measurement of results achieved against the standards and linking of rewards, discipline, and other personnel actions to the level of performance indicated by the measurement.

The performance of all managers must be measured and it must be measured in a highly sophisticated manner that insures accuracy and equity. Organization health depends upon it. How then, can this be accomplished?

Measuring by Objectives

As applied to measuring managers, what is probably the most effective approach is now commonly termed measuring by results or measuring by objectives. In essence, this approach provides that each manager will have an approved set of objectives that he is responsible for accomplishing during the measuring or target period. Most commonly, these objectives are set and reviewed on an annual basis. They constitute the manager's concrete job description and statement of accountability for the period under consideration.

There is little doubt that the better method for setting objectives is the one in which the objectives are drafted and recommended by the individual managers and then approved by their superiors. Once approved they become (1) the manager's directive of required action, and (2) the standards against which he will be measured—and rewarded or removed.

One of the most critical aspects of measuring by objectives is the superior's evaluation of the objectives against which the manager will perform and be measured. Again, it must be emphasized in this type of measurement that the objective must be set in advance. Thus the superior must evaluate each objective in terms of:

1. Does the objective represent a sufficient task for the manager during the measurement period?
2. Is the objective practical and attainable?
3. Is the objective clearly stated in terms of the task, the measuring period, and, the measurement method to be used?
4. Is the objective compatible with the organization's overall objectives and plans for the period?

Only after the superior has answered these questions is he in a position to pass upon the objective. If a "too easy" objective is approved (one that is too easily attainable or is an insufficient task for the measuring period) the organization will suffer in two ways. Number one, the organization will not have received due value for the period and, two, the manager's development has been impeded because he has not been provided with a proper goal to spur his performance—his objective has contributed to substandard performance.

Specific Objectives a Must

The word "standard" implies preciseness or a specific nature. Hence if objectives are to serve their intended purpose, the importance of making them specific cannot be overemphasized. If they are general or nebulous, they fail as a standard and effective measuring becomes impossible. Two examples will illustrate this point.

Example No. 1. Assume that both a division head and his department head were shortsighted enough to set an objective that reads: "The division manager's objective is to make a substantial improvement in the efficiency of his department during 1975." This alleged objective is subject to so many interpretations and misunderstandings that there is no way to evaluate when or if it has been reached. Thus his accomplishment cannot be measured.

Contrast that objective with one that reads: "Reduce the cost of operating his division during 1975 by $100,000 without eliminating any of the 12 major services currently provided."

Example No. 2. A poor, rather useless objective would read: "Increase the reading comprehension of fourth-grade students." Again, this is a general statement of intent. At best, it's a goal, not a specific statement of an end result. It contains an unknown factor. What is meant by "increasing the reading comprehension"? We remove the x factor when we define specifically what level of increase in comprehension is being sought. Removing the x factor and defining the specific intent is the prime method of changing a goal to a specific objective that can be measured and evaluated. A better objective might read: "During the next semester, increase the reading comprehension of 90 percent of the fourth-grade students by one skill level."

The Rating Process

Once the commitment has been made to measure by results, the actual rating process becomes both more accurate and more meaningful, and the entire process is facilitated.

The only form needed is simple, usually one page in length, which is vertically divided in half. At the beginning of the measuring period (for example, January 1 for the year 1975), the left side of the form contains a list of the specific objectives that the manager must accomplish during the measuring period. Both the subordinate and the superior are thoroughly familiar with these objectives, and both agree as to the specific meaning of the objectives. Figure 12 is a results-oriented evaluation form.

At the end of the measuring period (for example, December 31 for the year 1975), the superior moves to the right side of the page, and opposite each objective writes in the results that were

Figure 12. Results-oriented evaluation form, director, state employment
agency.

Objectives	Measure	Results Achieved			
		Quarters*			Total Year
		1st	2nd	3rd	
1. Improve by 10 percent number of qualified applicants referred for job openings.	1. At least three qualified candidates referred for each job opening.	T	O	T	Achieved in 97 percent of cases
2. Increase by 15 percent number of qualified welders during 1975.	2. Number of persons completing basic welding course #5.	O	T	T	17 completed course.

*Codes facilitating management by exception: T = On target. No action necessary
O = Off target. Action necessary

actually achieved by the manager during the measuring period.

Once the form has been completed at the end of the rating period the manager's performance becomes obvious and few mental gymnastics are necessary to determine how effective he was. The left side of the form says, "Here's what he should have done." The right side says, "Here's what he did." This, then, becomes the basis for discussion with the manager.

Much like measuring on the basis of results as contrasted to the traditional way, the discussion with the manager who has been rated will be dramatically different. Instead of not knowing what to expect, chances are the manager will know almost exactly how he has performed before the boss even opens his mouth. After all, the manager knows exactly what was expected of him and certainly has been keeping track of his own progress toward his objectives.

Thus the appraisal interview has become job-centered rather than personality-oriented. Instead of wasting time sparring with each other over immaterial factors, both superior and subordinate can get right down to brass tacks and constructively discuss the results and ways to improve them. Neither the boss nor the manager is ill at ease, because they do not have to discuss personalities and nebulous factors in the atmosphere that almost always prevailed with traditional measuring.

A few simple, easily applied checks can quickly tell an organization how effective its evaluation process is. Those organizations that rank low on the audit would be well advised to get their measuring house in order. The most important of these checkpoints include:

Extent of use. Once completed, what are the ratings used for? Are they merely filed, or are they constantly referred to for the purposes mentioned earlier in this article?

Orientation. Do the ratings concentrate on measuring results actually achieved, or are they oriented to personality factors that bear little resemblance to the results for which the manager is being held accountable?

Length of recording form. While the number of uses to which the rating is put will exert an impact on the length of the rating form, it is questionable whether any results-oriented rating form need consume more space than the front and back of one piece of paper. Any longer forms should be reviewed to make certain that quantity isn't being substituted for quality.

Specific versus general. It is mandatory that all ratings be completed in language that is as specific as possible. All ratings should describe specific accomplishments, not hopes, aspirations, and effort expended.

Connection with rewards. Does the management group have the conviction that the good and bad things they will receive from management life are determined primarily by the evaluation process, which in turn reflects the positive results they contribute or fail to contribute to the progress of the enterprise? If not, it's doubtful that the best performers will ever really appreciate the merits of the measuring process.

Correlation with reality. The acid test of all measuring processes must be the degree to which the ratings jibe both with the results managers achieve and with the competence of managers. If, in actual practice, the glowing words on a rating form are not matched by a manager's real performance, the measuring process is inadequate. Ratings must do more than indicate that 90 percent of the managers are warmhearted and true-blue.

This chapter will generally be of more benefit and will be more applicable to nongovernment organizations. Unfortunately, many government organizations are faced with overcoming a long history of evaluating managers on effort expended rather than on results achieved, on personality traits rather than on results. This is one of the main reasons why some government organizations are justifiably criticized as being more interested in efficiency (largely the way efforts are expended) rather than effectiveness (whether a worthwhile objective was attained by the effort). Fortunately, some government organizations, such as the Federal Office of Manpower and Budget, have raised serious questions regarding the traditional ways of evaluating managerial performance, and attempts—currently too early to analyze—are moving more toward results-oriented appraisals. The town of Wellesley, Massachusetts, presently evaluates its managers on a results basis and even pays them incentive compensation based on their results. A similar approach is used for senior officers of the Canadian armed forces. Hopefully, the trend will continue and accelerate. It will do much to bring a higher level of commitment and achievement to government managers.

DISCUSSION CASE
Alternative Approaches to Evaluating Managers

Organization A utilizes a results-oriented approach to performance appraisal. Its policy provides that the performance of each manager will be evaluated annually on the designated appraisal form. Following this, an appraisal interview is conducted between the manager and his boss. Emphasis in these interviews is on reviewing and discussing the strong and weak points of the manager's performance during the preceding year as well as discussing ways in which the manager may improve. The manager's compensation is not discussed during these sessions.

Organization B also follows a results-oriented approach. However, its policy provides for formal reviews between the manager and his boss at quarterly intervals during the year. At the end of the complete year, they discuss the manager's performance for the entire year. The manager's compensation is discussed with him during this session.

DISCUSSION POINTS

1. Which approach would normally be more conducive to increased motivation and performance?
2. List the strong and weak points of each approach.

8

Potential Pitfalls
in MBO

MBO can be deceptively simple. Managers, especially those who are novices to the system, can be lulled into expecting too much from it and failing to give adequate attention to recognizing and coping with its many potential pitfalls. I hope that nonprofit organizations won't make as many mistakes as corporations did as they evolved their approaches to MBO.

It is neither necessary nor desirable for nonprofit managers to "reinvent the wheel" when identifying these pitfalls. Definite patterns have developed in the installations made to date. This chapter discusses the more prevalent of these pitfalls. To managers considering adoption of an MBO system, the list may be helpful in planning; for organizations that have already embraced MBO and have experienced only limited success, it should serve as a debugging checklist. For still other organizations that latched on to MBO as a showpiece or because someone else had it, the list will be a handy guide as to why things went wrong.

Implementing in Ignorance

The widespread adoption and increasing popularity of MBO have tempted some organizations into adopting MBO without knowing what is really involved and the impact it will have on their organizations. Often, these organizations mistakenly believe that MBO is a panacea and that not to adopt it would be foolhardy.

A large credit union, with one of the more autocratic of senior management groups, implemented MBO in this pig-in-a-poke fashion. Only after having spent many frustrating months, and driving many dedicated managers to distraction, did this organization learn that MBO was completely incompatible with its management style and operating methods.

Management could have avoided much of this planned failure if it had first learned what MBO was all about and what changes it probably would necessitate in the organization and then determined whether the system was desirable.

Implementing in Haste

The early American Indian was often accused of believing that if a little medicine was good, more was better—a pitfall often encountered in MBO. One of the major "time shocks" of MBO is the amount of time required to make it effective in an organization. Usually, three to five years is required to reach what I term an 85 percent effectiveness level, the point at which most of the system is in place and being practiced by almost all managers. (The remaining 15 percent consists of the debugging and continual refining that must always accompany a successful implementation.)

One of the largest of government organizations, faced with strong demands for more significant results, tried to implement through four successive levels of management within a period of six months. Predictably, the result was wholesale confusion, lack of faith on the part of managers, and very little benefit gained from six months of expensive, feverish activity by many key personnel. The problem was compounded because many of the personnel were trained in specialties, not in management. Suddenly, they were erroneously considered to be managers capable of quickly installing a tough, demanding, total system of managing.

After management first determines whether MBO should be

installed, the next most critical question to be answered is, "How fast can and should the implementation proceed?"

Failing to Order Priorities

A frequent failing of nonprofit organizations is to become extremely busy without having first determined what all the busyness should be aimed at. This is one reason why they are often guilty of emphasizing efficiency over effectiveness. As an example, one hospital was actively pursuing six major efficiency studies. However, the hospital hadn't really established concrete objectives based on priorities. This is a contradictory situation as it often results in becoming increasingly efficient at something that shouldn't be done in the first place.

MBO is a potent means of lining up the efforts of all managers to achieve the overall objectives and priorities of the organization. Thus if the wrong priorities are set at any level, it means that a highly efficient approach is being misused.

Getting busy without having first determined priorities is like the airplane pilot who takes off without having determined his destination. He may fly the plane well (efficiency) but if he doesn't have a destination, he won't reach it (effectiveness).

Overemphasizing Objectives

As I have stressed, objectives become meaningful only if they operate within a system of management that insures that they are properly written in the first place and, once written, that they get translated into action that results in a living, viable way of managing the organization. Too often, objectives are stressed to the detriment of the system. When this occurs, managers are usually required to "come up with a list of objectives." The necessary preliminary work is not done. Objectives, thus, are written in a vacuum and usually aren't worth the paper they are written on. Often the list is filed away until the time arrives to write objectives for the next year. Managers don't use them as a way of managing and as a guide to action.

The overstressing of objectives is especially prevalent in those organizations that implement too quickly and in ignorance of the system.

Ignoring Feedback

The more motivated and achievement-oriented a manager is, the more he requires and demands feedback on his performance. He wants to continually know how well he's achieving his objectives. He's not content to remain in the dark.

One of the larger government agencies installed an operational planning system that, as far as it went, was excellent. The problem was that it didn't go far enough. All managers were required to submit objectives for the target period. Also, they were required to program out the step-by-step action by which they planned to achieve their objectives. Both of these steps were excellent, and the managers in general pursued them with diligence. However, no method of feedback was developed to permit them to monitor their progress as the objectives and plans unfolded. Very quickly, the managers came to regard their objectives as just an exercise in writing; they never knew how well they were performing and so they treated the system as something that took a lot of time and effort but resulted in nothing but paperwork. Today, the operational planning system is a dirty word in that agency.

Failing to Reward Managers

No management system will be effective if it continually emphasizes higher levels of performance and improvement but fails to reward and recognize the managers for their higher performance levels. Rewards should equal performance.

Considerable attention must be devoted to developing rewards and recognition for nonprofit managers. This is especially true in government organizations, where usually there is less flexibility to utilize compensation as a method of rewarding. In two MBO installations in the nonprofit sector—one in a large church and one in the Department of Defense—the basic assumption was made that compensation payments could not provide enough flexibility. The managers of both these organizations explored all other alternative methods of recognizing performance. The church organization developed 88 alternative ways, and the DOD unit arrived at over a hundred ways. These alternative methods ranged from a verbal pat on the back to time off with pay. Given the lack of flexibility in many organizations, no avenue of providing recognition can be left unexplored.

Failing to Program Objectives

Even the best written objective will seldom be achieved if left to chance. The manager must plan out the step-by-step action for achieving the objective. This is one of the major ways by which objectives are translated into a day-to-day means of managing.

Yet the failure to require managers to program out their objectives continues to be one of the major pitfalls in MBO. An effective MBO system gives equal recognition to the plans to support the objective as it does to the objectives themselves. Experience has demonstrated that objectives without plans are largely myths or delusions. The following problems result when plans are not developed to achieve the objective:

1. The objective cannot be tested for realism.
2. It is all but impossible to intelligently allocate resources to the objective.
3. The manager has no guide or timetable for action during the target period.
4. Monitoring or controlling of progress becomes extremely difficult.

Omitting Periodic Reviews

The more successful MBO systems feature periodic reviews—usually at quarterly intervals—during the target period. The purposes of these reviews are to measure performance, to review the validity of the original objective, and to take remedial action, if necessary, while there is still time left during the target period.

MBO can be dealt a lethal blow by omitting these reviews. Neither the supervisor nor his subordinate will know how the other is performing until the final review at the end of the target period, when there will be no opportunity to take corrective action. Without interim reviews on a formal basis and according to a definite schedule, any detection of varying performance will be as much a matter of luck as of plan.

The use of quarterly reviews during the target period, instead of just one final one at the end of the year, changes much of the emphasis from one at looking back at a year that is already past to one of looking ahead at the rest of the year while something can still be done about it.

Omitting Refresher Training

Many organizations do a highly commendable training and orientation job when MBO is first installed. The training, though, ends at that point, and managers who are new to the system are left to secure their MBO training through a combination of osmosis and hit-or-miss tutoring by the older hands—who may or may not be competent teachers. Changes and refinements to the original system are handled in much the same way.

This is an excellent way to kill the system, since the first three years following the installation of an MBO program constitute a period of continuous tailoring and refining of the system. After three years, the original system may have been changed by as much as 50 percent, and only the most informal retraining has been conducted.

Delegating Executive Direction

Without exception, every successful MBO system has borne continuously, from its first day of implementation, the clear and unmistakable mark of the top manager in charge. This involvement by the top manager cannot be delegated.

Notable failures have occurred when attempts were made to delegate the executive direction to other departments, such as personnel. The system often becomes known as just another "personnel gimmick," which can't be too important because the top man discontinued his intimate involvement with it. A total way of managing an organization—which is what MBO is—cannot be delegated. It would be tantamount to a manager's saying that he doesn't want to manage.

Overconceptualizing

With MBO there are two major potential problems—overconceptualizing and creating a papermill.

The trap of overconceptualizing can occur when too much attention is paid to techniques, procedures, and skills. One MBO system in a school organization is so complicated that the principals and administrators have been provided with several pages, really a small dictionary, of terms, which they must master. Over a page and a half is devoted to the subtle differences between an objective and a goal. Instead, they should be devoting their time and attention to the analysis, thinking, and planning that are the heart of MBO.

Paperwork is another potential trap. Some ineffective MBO systems fill manual after manual with forms, procedures, and other time wasters. MBO managers should be analysis-oriented not method-oriented. A strict control should be exercised over every form and piece of paper built into the system. Properly handled, MBO usually results in a small amount of high-quality paperwork.

Emphasizing Short-Term Objectives

A rather prevalent weakness in many nonprofit organizations is the tendency to concentrate primarily upon the immediate future without having formulated long-term objectives and plans. Many government organizations fund on an annual or a two-year basis. School budgets frequently cover one year. Volunteer organizations usually live from year to year.

Many of the needs these organizations are trying to meet can be met only on a long-term basis. Thus when the annual or short-term period is overemphasized, these organizations can't be certain they are meeting the long-range needs. This probably accounts to a large degree for the large number of program starts and stops. Continuity, expressed first in long-term objectives, followed by short-term ones, is much needed.

Emphasizing Programs Over Objectives

Many government units are guilty of practicing "programitis"; they get busy administering programs before they determine their objectives. This often leads to the feverish carrying out of activities without regard to the results the programs and projects should accomplish. Programs and projects should be regarded as the plans by which a predetermined objective is to be reached. If the objective is not set first, the cart is before the horse.

Playing the Numbers Game

Another major pitfall is the overemphasis on numbers as a means of measuring success without first having determined the need to be met. Often, nonprofit organizations have equated success with the level of funding they succeeded in getting this year versus last year. As an example, the fact that twice as much was spent on Boy Scout activities for 1974 over 1973 is no assurance that the organization was twice as successful. The numbers don't indicate the real need that was to be met or how it was met. If a city increases its police officers by 50 percent but the crime rate goes up 20 percent, there is a major question as to whether the real need is being met.

To avoid the numbers trap, more attention must be devoted to determining the real social needs to be met and then expressing those needs in terms of specific, prioritized objectives.

All the above pitfalls pose serious stumbling blocks to the success of MBO. Of course, no manager actually starts an MBO program with the goal of destroying it. However, the injurious impact to MBO is the same whether the manager fails through ignorance or by design.

MBO is a tough, demanding management system whose operation requires highly competent managers. By paying attention to the problem areas set forth in this book, managements can increase the effectiveness and value of the MBO programs that they have implemented or plan to implement.

DISCUSSION CASE
Pitfalls in Writing Objectives

During October 1974, after attending a three-day seminar on MBO and reading several articles and a book on the subject, the top management group of your organization has decided to implement MBO for 1975. On November 4, your boss provides you with the following information and assignment:

1. He is required to present his objectives to his boss by December 1.
2. He requests that you recommend to him, by December 1, five objectives for your job for 1975.
3. Your objectives should be high-priority ones.
4. Your objectives should be realistic and attainable.
5. The objectives that you recommend must make a substantial contribution to the organization's progress during 1975.
6. You must be committed to carrying out the objectives on a can-and-will-do basis.

7. Your boss suggests that it would be helpful to you to read one of the well-recognized books on management by objectives.

DISCUSSION POINTS

1. Briefly describe how you would go about carrying out the assignment from your boss.
2. Briefly describe any problems you think you might encounter.

9

Benefits
to the Manager

Any approach to management that does not benefit the manager and help him manage his job more efficiently and effectively is the wrong management system for him. MBO is no exception.

Fortunately, MBO is capable of delivering many well-proven benefits to the manager. However, the words "capable of delivering" are used advisedly. How many of the benefits the manager will enjoy, and the degree to which he will enjoy them, are conditioned by several factors: how thoroughly the implementation was made, the management style of the organization and the extent of its commitment to MBO, and the manager's own competence and motivation. All three of these are major variables.

The following paragraphs outline the benefits more commonly experienced. They have become practical realities to many managers already practicing MBO. They should be the goals that managers newly embarking on their MBO efforts should strive for.

Greater Voice in Determining the Job

Rather than being told what to do or being the recipient of job assignments, under MBO the manager is given the greatest practical latitude to determine his job. Normally, he is made aware of the organization's overall requirements by being apprised of the higher-level objectives and priorities that he must help carry out. With these higher-level requirements as his guide, he makes his own recommendations, in the form of his suggested objectives and plans, as to what part he should play in achieving them. Through the link-pin team approach discussed earlier, he also has a voice in helping determine the higher-level objectives. Thus he has a major voice through two avenues in determining much of his own job.

More Self-Management

Once the manager has reached agreement with his superior as to what the manager must accomplish (his objectives), how he plans to accomplish them (his plans to achieve his objectives), and the resources he will require to accomplish his objectives, the manager should be able to manage his department with a fairly high degree of autonomy. In the absence of MBO, he must frequently run to his superior to request approval of what he should do, how he should do it, and how much money he should spend.

More Self-Supervision

This benefit is much related to self-managing. Oversupervising frequently occurs when there has been no clear-cut agreement on what is expected of a subordinate. The amount of supervision should decrease in proportion to the degree agreement has been reached on the results required and the target date by which the results must be achieved. This is logical. If a superior doesn't know what a subordinate is doing, the superior will almost invariably check on him at frequent intervals; in turn the subordinate will doubt if he is really in charge.

More Self-Control and Discipline

There are two methods of controlling and disciplining. In one, the superior receives most of the meaningful feedback on the subordinate's performance, and the superior is the prime mover when corrective action or change is called for. Often, the subordinate must wait to take action until his superior tells him to. The weakness of this approach is that the initiative is on the back of the superior—not the subordinate, who is supposed to be in charge. Secondly, considerable delay often results when the subordinate must wait to be told when action is necessary.

Under MBO, control and monitoring reports are designed primarily for the subordinate's use. In addition to causing corrective action to be determined nearer the scene of the action, this places the initiative on the subordinate's shoulders. When he knows something has gone wrong, he can take action without waiting to be told. Again, he's enjoying more self-management.

Agreement on What Is Expected

Several studies have indicated that, in the absence of clearly defined job requirements, there is considerable confusion between superior and subordinate as to what is required of the subordinate. This frequently results in the subordinate's operating in the dark and being criticized for matters that he didn't understand.

MBO should provide every manager with better understanding of what is required of him. It should also minimize criticism for matters that are not his responsibility.

Appraisal and Rewards Based on Results

Nonprofit managers frequently gripe that no matter how hard they work they receive little credit. MBO insists that managers be appraised on the basis of their objectives and the degree to which they were achieved. This benefit of MBO should be especially welcome to the dedicated nonprofit manager who for so long has been judged on factors other than results and who has found it impossible to receive proper credit for his accomplishments.

Following on the heels of appraisal based on results is rewards based on results. The two are inseparable.

MBO makes it possible to single out the outstanding performer from the average or mediocre ones. In so doing it provides what is probably the only equitable basis for rewarding and recognizing managers. In the absence of clearly defined objectives and evaluation of performance, management frequently grants promotions, compensation, and other rewards to the deserving and the undeserving in relatively equal amounts.

Prevention of "Continual Absorption"

Managers in nonprofit organizations, especially those in government, are plagued by what they term "continual absorption." Higher levels continue to add more and more work and programs to the manager's day without due regard to the work he already has and before long any semblance of priority has been confused or hopelessly lost. The manager ends up juggling too many balls.

Under MBO, the manager's objectives are based on agreed-upon priorities. Say, for example, a manager has seven objectives for the target period. A higher level comes to him and tells him he must take on several new programs. Pointing to his objectives and the workload necessary to accomplish them, he can justify his inability to "absorb" any more projects. If the new projects have a higher priority, then he can demonstrate that some of his present objectives will have to be deprioritized to permit him to take on the new workload.

In the absence of objectives, it is extremely difficult for a manager to justify, both to his superior and to himself, his ability or inability to take on more work.

Better Management of Time

MBO insists that the important be separated from the routine. It insists that all effort be directed toward previously determined results; effort is not expended until the objective has been determined. Thus MBO helps the manager avoid what has been referred to as the activity trap or the time trap.

MBO should help nonprofit organizations overcome one of the most frequent criticisms against them; namely, that they concentrate too much on efficiency without proper regard to effectiveness. A good example of the activity trap is law enforcement officers attempting to control crime by increasing the number of patrols from six to eight without having first determined if patrols are the best way to control crime.

Fewer Surprises

One of the truisms of management is that the fewer the surprises the better the management. Another way to express this is that the more the unexpected can be anticipated and planned for, the more effective management will be. The alternative is management by crisis and decision by expediency.

MBO carries with it a future orientation. It requires managers to look beyond today and plan for the future. The courses of action the manager lays out helps him minimize the surprises. The monitoring and feedback aspects of MBO help him spot trouble at the earliest possible time, so that quick action is possible when a surprise does develop.

Greater Commitment and Motivation

All available evidence indicates that managers are more highly committed and motivated when they have definite objectives to work toward, when they know where they're going, when they receive feedback on their performance, when they are judged on results, and when they are rewarded on the basis of results. MBO provides all these, and the least effective manager probably is the one to whom these opportunities have been denied.

Better Communication and Coordination

MBO forces both of these. Unless managers are to write their objectives in a vacuum, they must know what higher levels plan to accomplish during the target period, what will take place in other departments and units, and how the manager's job fits into the total picture. What balance must be observed between the manager's objectives and plans and those of other managers and units? What must the manager do for others; what must they do for him? Such questions must be answered if MBO is to help improve results and not just end up as a laundry list of objectives.

Better Management Development

It is now commonly accepted that effective management development takes place on the job and that it is largely self-development. MBO has many qualities that meet these two premises. Each manager is held accountable for a meaningful job and the results. He is continually encouraged to stand up and be counted—to recommend his objectives and to plan out how he'll achieve them. He's called upon to make decisions within his authority, and he knows what authority he has. When his objectives or plans don't work out, he's primarily responsible for formulating corrective action. Finally, he knows he'll be judged on what he accomplishes, rather than on what he says he can do. All these factors, by placing the initiative squarely on the back of the manager, provide the real guts of management development. In doing so, they continually prepare the manager for greater responsibility and rewards.

Greater Job Satisfaction

With so much attention on the need for job enrichment at the nonmanagerial level, it is easy to overlook the alarming evidence of the job dissatisfaction at the managerial level, especially among middle managers.

Job dissatisfaction among managers in many nonprofit organizations is rampant. Many nonprofit managers look upon themselves not as managers but as administrators or "carry-outers" of matters over which only the top levels are truly managers. They see themselves as having little authority and even less discretion. They see their jobs bounded and prescribed by volumes of detailed operating procedures that require them to be more adept at reading than at managing.

Over 20 years of experience with MBO has demonstrated its benefit as a down-to-earth means of enriching managerial jobs in the private sector.[1] Experience to date indicates that the pursuit of this benefit may be even more important in the nonprofit sector. Certainly the depth of the need is apparent.

[1] See Dale D. McConkey, "Enriching the Manager's Job Through MBO," *Management by Objectives Journal,* September 1973.

Greater Respect for Nonprofit Managers

Not to be overlooked when citing the benefits of MBO is the possibility it offers the nonprofit manager for gaining increased acceptance and respect from those who are currently his critics. Although it is usually wrong and unfair, the fact remains that the nonprofit manager suffers from a severe form of stereotyping. He's often viewed as an incompetent who chose a nonprofit organization because he couldn't survive in a corporation. He's considered to lack ambition and motivation. He's believed to be primarily interested in coasting along at an easy pace until the time arrives for him to receive what is commonly viewed as being a lucrative pension. Certainly, many nonprofit managers do fall into these categories, but the same types are also found in the corporate world.

However, the vast majority of the nonprofit managers with whom I have become acquainted are competent, dedicated managers. If as a group they are guilty of anything, it is not having the proper means and methods for demonstrating their mettle and contributions. Hopefully, MBO will provide the means and methods for those who are dedicated to its application. To the extent nonprofit managers are successful in its application, they are certain to bring some rude awakenings to, and evoke better appreciation from, their critics.

This chapter was purposely written from the viewpoint of benefits to the individual manager. He has the right to (and should) ask, "What's in it for me?" However, the reader shouldn't overlook the benefits to the organization as a whole.

The total organization, which is the ultimate beneficiary of these combined and cumulative benefits to its managers, certainly enjoys the opportunity for success of a magnitude far above the organization whose managers are deprived of these same benefits. It may be trite, but definitely appropriate, to remind us all that an organization is the sum total of its components.

Lest I be accused of being an idealist, let me reemphasize an earlier point. Not every manager in every organization can expect to receive 100 percent of any or all of the benefits cited in this chapter. However, there should be goals to seek and actively work for. The potential is there in each of them to be capitalized on by the organization that will put forth the required efforts in the MBO system.

DISCUSSION CASE
Rewarding Performance

Most authorities on motivation agree that recognition of performance is one of the prime means of maintaining motivation. Rewards, including compensation, form an important part of recognition.

Many nonprofit organizations, especially those in government operations, do not enjoy the flexibility to change their compensation plans to place them more on a results-oriented basis. These organizations must place more emphasis on noncompensation forms of recognition. Those managers who determine rewards policies should give considerable thought to the discussion points below.

DISCUSSION POINTS

1. Can the compensation plans (salary, incentives, benefits) be changed to make payments in substantially different amounts to managers on the basis of the results they achieve?
2. If the answer to Question No. 1 is "Yes," what changes would be conducive to increased recognition and motivation?
3. If the answer to Question No. 1 is "No":
   (a) First, make a list of all practical means of recognizing performance except those involving compensation payments.
   (b) Evaluate each item on the list in terms of its impact on motivating better performance.
   (c) Determine which items are most practical to implement.

10

Implementing MBO

Not all MBO applications have been successful. Some have been resounding successes; others have been outright failures. The success of others is questionable. Why?

Almost invariably the answer lies in the manner in which the system was implemented and especially in the pre-implementation phase. A study of the implementation methods as related to later success indicates a high degree of correlation in more than 300 different MBO programs. The organizations that understood the full import of MBO and took the time and effort required to implement it properly have enjoyed the maximum fruits of the system. Those that devoted only minimal time and effort to implementation have enjoyed success only commensurate with their efforts.

The organizations that endeavored to adopt and copy the system out of hand, and overnight, have usually failed. The strongest support for these conclusions is that not one single company that properly implemented the system in the first instance has ever discontinued using it as its primary approach to management. Certainly, these organizations modified and amended their systems as experience was gained, but the basic MBO system is still intact and being vigorously pursued. Thus it becomes of paramount importance to define "implementation" and to set forth its key components. Of equal importance is a complete understanding of the prerequisites management must meet before it begins to implement the system.

There remains little question that the MBO system has received numerous, undeserved black eyes. Almost all these black eyes should have been visited upon the managers who tried to adopt the system without being competent to do so. Contrary to belief in some quarters, MBO is not a simple system. It has many principles, many nuances—some subtle, some overt—many virtues, and many pitfalls. All must be understood, appreciated, and practiced by the manager who would apply it successfully.

Before the Implementation

Much of the success of implementation should be based on a major question that must always precede implementation: Do we really understand what MBO is all about and do we want to adopt it in our organization? Too many organizations, much to their regret, have moved right into implementation without having carefully considered this question. The top manager, and hopefully his senior managers, will complete an exhaustive analysis before making their decision. The analysis will include securing definitive answers to several critical questions, which include:

1. Do we really understand the full import of MBO as it would affect our organization? Do we understand how it operates, its strengths, its pitfalls?

2. Is it right for our organization? Are we willing to devote the time and effort (especially on the part of the top people) to make it effective (probably a minimum of three years to reach 85 percent effectiveness)?

3. Are we ready for it? Have we met the three major prerequisites—proper management atmosphere, organizational clarity, and an effective management information system? If not, can we meet them before implementation?

4. Is this the better timing? Are operations so unstable pres-

ently that there would be an excessive number of distractions from the concerted effort required? Will sufficient managerial time be available? Would another period be better?

5. Why do we want it, what will it do for our organization? Various aids are available to assist in this analysis phase. They include—again, as a very minimum—the following:

Reading. Several excellent books are available, written by recognized professionals, but check out the person before buying the book. Those books that include actual case studies are especially valuable, as the organizations discussed can serve as the basis for further investigation as suggested below. Time spent on researching and preparing a bibliography will be well worthwhile.

Experience of other organizations. Properly undertaken, this phase will provide the better basis for making a decision. Ask penetrating questions of at least six organizations that have practiced MBO for at least three years, and insist on full answers. Are they really practicing MBO or claiming to for window dressing? What have been their successes and failures? What impact did it have on their management group and overall performance? For what purposes do they use MBO? What conditions prevailed in the organization? Would they do it over again?

Outside counsel. Finally, bring in competent (repeat, *competent*) outside help on an ad hoc basis to answer questions and provide guides and checkpoints for your decision.

The ultimate question to be answered is: *Are you certain of what you are getting involved in, and are you fully committed to making MBO work in your organization?* Only if this question can be answered in the affirmative, without reservation, should an organization move to the implementation stage.

The Major Variables

Three of the more common approaches for implementing MBO are discussed later in this chapter. The implementation approach that is finally decided upon and the time and effort required to make the actual implementation will be heavily influenced by several major variables.

Size of organization. This variable centers around the sheer weight of numbers and scale. For example, implementation in a gigantic organization like the Department of Health, Education, and Welfare (with a fiscal year budget of $115 billion) is infinitely more complex than for a community fund entity with an annual budget of $200,000.

Number of managers. Will 5,000 managers be involved or only a handful?

Organization structure. Is the structure flat, having only three or four levels of management? Or is it steep, having possibly eight to ten levels?

Variety of services. For obvious reasons, it is usually much easier to implement in an organization providing only one major service to a limited client group than in one providing a wide diversity of services to diverse client groups.

Geographical dispersion. Distances between locations of various branch offices and managers' difficulty in communicating and meeting with one another contribute to the time and effort resulting from this variable.

Homogeneity of management group. Usually, implementation will be facilitated by the degree to which managers share common backgrounds and qualifications such as education, experience, and disciplines.

Relationship with governing body. This variable gets involved to a considerable degree with the question of how much autonomy the operating managers enjoy with respect to their governing body. Does the governing body get heavily involved in the day-to-day operations of the organization? For example, in some hospitals it is difficult to determine who is actually operating it—the board of trustees or the administrator.

Historical interests. Often, this is one of the more frustrating variables to evaluate and cope with. Suffice it to say that the more historical or landed interests, or "empires," which must be dealt with, the more difficult and time-consuming the implementation will be.

Management style. The more successful MBO systems are accompanied by what is commonly referred to as the participative management style. The farther away the organization's management style is from the participative style, the more time and work required to implement MBO. People must accept and be trained in a different management style.

Supportive structure. Every management style is accompanied by a definite structure designed to support that management style. This structure includes components like authority, decision making, planning, communications, feedback, and policies.

Changing the existing supporting structure to tailor it to an MBO style of managing can take considerable time and resources.

Three Common Approaches

Figure 13 summarizes the three most prevalent approaches to implementation, and outlines the major features to be evaluated prior to selecting the appropriate approach for a particular organization. It will be noted rather quickly that the major differences in the three approaches revolve around the degree to which top management is sold on and committed to MBO, the speed with which implementation proceeds, and the number of managers and managerial levels involved at any given time. For example, in an organization having an enthusiastic, highly committed top management, the implementation often is completed in one to two years and all levels become actively involved almost from the very beginning. In contrast, one having a more conservative management may spread the implementation over three or four years, and only a relatively few managers become involved in the beginning, with the number increasing gradually as implementation moves to succeeding levels.

Effectiveness of Each Approach

Figure 13 indicates that success is tied closely to the speed of the implementation, with the lowest probable success accompanying the implementation when all levels of management are brought into the system at the same time and the installation is compressed into a short time span. While several successful installations have been made in this fashion, they are the exception rather than the rule. The managers involved have been typified in the "Type of Management to Which Suited" category.

There are several reasons why the "All Levels at Once" approach has a low probability of success. MBO is a way of life, it is a tough, demanding state of managerial thinking translated into action. Neither a way of life nor a way of thinking can be changed precipitately. Time for indoctrination and assimilation is required. Time also is required to understand the full import and impact of the system before trying to assimilate it—let alone implement it.

Figure 13. Guide for determining an implementation approach for MBO.

	APPROACH		
	One Level at a Time	*One Department Only*	*All Levels at Once*
General description	Implementation takes place one level (sometimes two) at a time starting at the top. Six months to a year is devoted to each level before moving to next level.	A "guinea pig" department runs a "pilot" test to decide whether or not MBO will be extended to other departments.	All levels of management are considered as a single group and MBO is implemented all at once for the entire group.
Type of organization to which suited	Large one with many managers and many levels of management. Many services. Geographically dispersed. Many client groups. Nonintegrated product or services.	Either large or small and of any type, but more frequently to larger ones with many diverse operations.	Smaller organizations. Few managers and few levels. Integrated service lines. Geographically concentrated.
Type of management to which suited	Emphasizes long-term growth. Methodical. Conservative. Not oriented to objectives.	Doubting Thomas. Little, if any, exposure to MBO. Often wedded to the past. Slow to try new approaches. Very conservative.	Gung ho. Homogeneous group. Objectives-oriented. Skilled at delegation. Accustomed to dealing with disciplines. Highly educated managers.
Time required by top management (during implementation)	Considerable but spread over a longer period of time.	*	Extensive, running several months. Considerable time also required later to debug the mistakes from moving very rapidly.
Time required by all managers (during implementation)	Average and spread over longer period of time.	*	Same, as above, for top management.

Top management commitment required	Average.	*	Full.
Implementation time required	Three to four years.	*	One to two years.
Advantages	In-depth understanding by each manager. More opportunity to debug as experience is gained. Each level becomes "teachers" for next level. System is more tailor-made to organization.	Mistakes are isolated. Provides "selling" tool for other departments. Results in a trained cadre of knowledgeable MBO managers.	Training duplication is minimized. Greater impact, faster. Higher immediate involvement of all managers.
Disadvantages	More time-consuming generally. Training is duplicated. Some levels are operating under MBO while others are not. Extensive top management time and effort are spent meeting with several levels. Temporary confusion and misunderstanding at lower levels if not communicated with.	Selection of right pilot department is critical. No assurance efforts are aimed to top needs of organization. Future MBO efforts will suffer unduly if limited experience is not successful. Usual risks from projecting from a small sample.	Few checks and balances on validity of objectives. Likelihood of autocratic actions to maintain pace. Blind lead the blind. Mistakes are multiplied. Likely to adopt a canned program rather than tailoring it. Usually requires outside help. Decisions based on expediency.
Outside help required	Average.	Minimal to average.	Extensive.
Dollar cost of implementing	Highest.	*	Lowest.
Probability of success	Highest.	Average.	Lowest.

* Depends upon which way the implementation proceeds after the "pilot" run, that is, one level at a time or all at once.

Source: Dale D. McConkey, "How to Succeed and Fail with MBO," *The Business Quarterly*, Winter 1974, p. 60.

The time constraint impacts even on small entities with only a few managers and levels of management, a lesson learned the hard way by a small volunteer organization in the Midwest. This organization, with an annual budget of less than $3 million and approximately 40 managers, crashed through an MBO installation in less than six months. Now, 18 months and many disappointments later, it still is struggling to establish a believable base with its managers so that it can begin implementing MBO the way it should have in the first place. Their task is not easy because it requires overcoming the disenchantment of each manager multiplied by 40 times. Conversely, one of the larger volunteer organizations spread its implementation over six years, proceeding one level at a time, and now enjoys the full fruits of its MBO labors. Neither the time span nor the approach was 100 percent responsible for this failure and success; however, the senior managers who were intimately involved in these two cases attribute much of the result to these two features of implementation.

Outside Counsel

The need for outside help increases with the speed of implementation. Invariably in the "All Levels at Once" approach it is necessary to make extensive use of outsiders who have gained their experience working with other organizations. Naturally, one of the more potentially unfavorable results is that the outsider may be advocating adoption of a system and principles that, although successful in other organizations, may require considerable varying, revising, and adapting for another organization. Tailoring requires time for investigating and analyzing. When this time is not made available, the result usually is a copycat plan, with many of the pertinent decisions based on expediency. An excessive amount of retraining and debugging time will be required later even if the implementation is successful. Usually it is preferable to take the additional time for implementation and as much as possible solve the problems and fully answer all questions before proceeding to the next stage. This requires continual deliberation by internal personnel, but it is time well spent.

Another problem that must be recognized when using outside counsel is the strong likelihood that the MBO system will become linked too closely with the consultant and managers will begin looking upon it as the consultant's program rather than the organization's. Any system that isn't regarded as the product and creation of the organization's leaders will be ineffective. The qualifications of an MBO consultant are covered later in this chapter.

Commitment

For managers to successfully achieve their objectives, they must be fully committed and motivated for top performance. Much of the key to getting them into this frame of mind is to insure that they understand the whys and benefits of MBO, both to their organizations and to them individually. Extreme care must be exercised, especially in the early days, to avoid leaving them with the negative impression that the system is primarily a device for pinning them with set accountabilities as a means of checking on them and possibly "hanging" them later on. The entire implementation stage must be approached in a positive manner. If an attempt is made to teach them only the mechanics of MBO, which usually happens in a speedy installation, they may well receive the system on a negative note.

Another compelling reason why the "One Level at a Time" approach is recommended for most installations is that managers become better indoctrinated in the rationale of the system and usually can witness its benefits as the implementation unfolds. In the faster installations, they must rely on blind faith that the system is of benefit and will work. They don't have the experience of the succeeding levels of management above them.

Top Management Time

Time required by top management is a major consideration when deciding which of the three approaches to follow. The top manager and his senior directors and department heads must devote a high percentage of their time, direction, and efforts to the installation. It cannot be handled by staff people or others acting in their behalf.

The time element compounds itself when the "All at Once" approach is selected. Not only must top management spend considerable time on the installation, but the time must be spent in solid blocks; that is, almost exclusive concentration on the installation is required while it is unfolding. Few top managers can devote their time without major problems arising in other areas of their responsibility.

Although the "One Level at a Time" approach will require greater total time because of duplicate training sessions and meetings with the several levels of management, the time need not be concentrated in a short period. Top managers can work on other matters in between the training sessions and follow-up meetings. This is one of the primary reasons why most organizations select the more gradual approach.

Organizational Clarity

The clearest possible organization must be structured. The salient feature of MBO is that the system comprises a 100 percent delegation for results; delegation poses the rather absolute requirement that the entity know who is responsible for what. Without exception, every MBO system unearths existing confusion as to job content and management accountability. This confusion must be resolved before proceeding with the next stage or management level during the implementation. This problem is resolved more effectively in the "One Level at a Time" approach. The reason would appear obvious. If there is organizational confusion at the top—say at the highest level—this confusion will be compounded down the line as the manager delegates to each of his subordinate levels. Proceeding one level at a time permits the confusion to be resolved at the higher level before being fanned out through the organization through the delegation process.

Using Consultants

The use of outside consultants to assist in implementing is often an unqualified disaster. This is unfortunate because the expertise of an outside consultant is frequently required. Failing to hire a competent consultant often leads an organization into the major pitfall of trying to master the MBO system itself and, at the same time, trying to apply it. This is an endeavor not unlike trying to study medicine and practice it concurrently.

However, caution is appropriate for those organizations that may require outside assistance. The rapid growth of MBO has brought with it the usual camp followers, soothsayers, and peddlers of magic. They take the form of consultants, business educators, and educational management associations. Practically every week someone else is publicly declaring himself to be an expert in MBO. And their ranks continue to grow, swelled as they are by the unqualified who read a few books on the subject, attend a session or two, and then hang out their shingles. Of such stuff "experts" and instant—but short-lived—heroes are made.

Those who may consider outside help would be well advised to seek definitive answers to the following questions before retaining assistance:

1. Has he had at least five years' experience working with all phases of MBO? Hopefully he will have been a key manager operating in an organization that practiced MBO.

2. Has he made at least one full-scale MBO installation and lived with it for a minimum of three years?

3. Does his experience include all phases of MBO treated as a total management system, or has he worked primarily with one or two facets of the total system; for example, planning and/or evaluation of performance? The specialist is like a duck out of water when trying to advise on the many aspects of an initial installation.

4. Did he get the bulk of his knowledge from practical experience, or is he quoting from a book or some quoter of quoters?

5. Does he talk practical language, or does he fill the air with definitions and high-priced terms? Does he preach or practice?

6. Can he give specific examples as to how each phase of MBO works?

7. Will he give you an introduction to the subject and a thick report of recommendations along with a big bill and then leave, or will he stay and work with you through the implementation stage by stage? The former should be avoided at all costs.

8. Is he knowledgeable when applying MBO to staff jobs, or is his experience confined to applications to line jobs, where the application is much easier?

9. Can he cite some of his work where MBO hasn't been 100 percent effective? If he's had the requisite experience, he's had a few of these.

10. Is he trying to peddle a large number of forms and paperwork? Does he insist that all forms must be used exactly as recommended? Excessive paperwork is a major weakness of MBO, and too many forms usually indicate a person who is more skilled in method than in analysis. MBO requires an analytical mind.

11. Is he worth at least the $800 to $1,000 a day he should be charging? A qualified practitioner is worth this. If he's not charging it, and earning it, he's probably the wrong man.

Indoctrinating Managers

As Approach 1, "One Level at a Time," is recommended by the preponderance of experience, it will be used in the remainder of this chapter when discussing the highlights of indoctrinating managers. It must be appreciated that these highlights provide only a guide and must be tailored to the individual organizations.

Implementation for each level is divided roughly into two periods of six months each—the first period consists of indoctrination and getting ready to operate, the second six months is devoted to actually operating under MBO on a dry-run basis.

The controlling rationale, especially during the first six months, should be to take small bites and digest each one completely before proceeding to the next. This is the foundation-laying stage and, much like constructing a building, a sound total structure cannot be built on a sloppy foundation.

Stage 1: Getting ready. This stage should cover MBO as a system and the writing of effective objectives. An objective should never be written until the writer understands the system in which the objective operates. Violation of this premise almost invariably results in uncoordinated objectives written in a vacuum and carried out in isolation rather than as a proportionate part of departmental and company objectives. Both the system and the objectives are covered by a combination of reading assignments, discussion groups, workshop sessions, and coaching by competent leaders.

After about two to three months of indoctrination, managers usually are prepared to start writing simple objectives. Emphasis should be devoted to getting managers accustomed to, and comfortable working with, objectives and the place of their objectives in the total scheme of things, not in writing grandiose objectives. That can come later.

During the ensuing three months, the intent is to have each manager write increasingly complex objectives, each writing followed by an evaluation and coaching session, until he has become fairly adept at structuring meaningful, measurable objectives. Finally, he recommends a group of objectives on which he will operate and be measured during the second six months—the dry-run phase.

Stage 2: Operating under objectives. It is made clear to each manager that he is operating under MBO on a dry-run basis during these six months and that his future will not sink or swim on the basis of his results. He is still undergoing training and indoctrination.

A feedback method is established to measure his performance against each of his objectives. Both he and his superior receive copies. Halfway through this stage the manager and his superior hold a formal review (just as they will do in the future for each quarter of the year) to evaluate progress toward objectives, discuss any variances, and review the validity of the objectives for the remainder of the period. Necessary revisions are made to plans and objectives.

A similar review takes place three months later (at the end of the full year) and if managers are found capable, they begin actually operating under all facets of MBO. The implementation then moves down to the next level of management, and similar indoctrination is provided. The process continues until all levels are covered and the total management group has become a part of MBO.

The importance of effective communication is emphasized during the transition from one stage to another. If the fact that MBO is being adopted is treated as a deep, dark secret, the levels of management yet to be covered will likely build up fear and distrust of the system. Managers at all levels should be acquainted with the fact that MBO is being adopted, and be given the timetable, the reasons why (purpose), and the part they will play in the system. Progress reports should be issued periodically and senior managers encouraged to brief their managers from time to time as the installation unfolds.

Figure 14 illustrates the indoctrination and implementation approach followed in a highly successful MBO installation in a large department of the Canadian federal government.

After the Implementation

No one has yet made a perfect installation. Nor will they!

Therefore, the final phase of implementation goes on forever to one degree or another. It consists of continually evaluating the

Figure 14. A model to implement and operate a total systems approach to MBO.

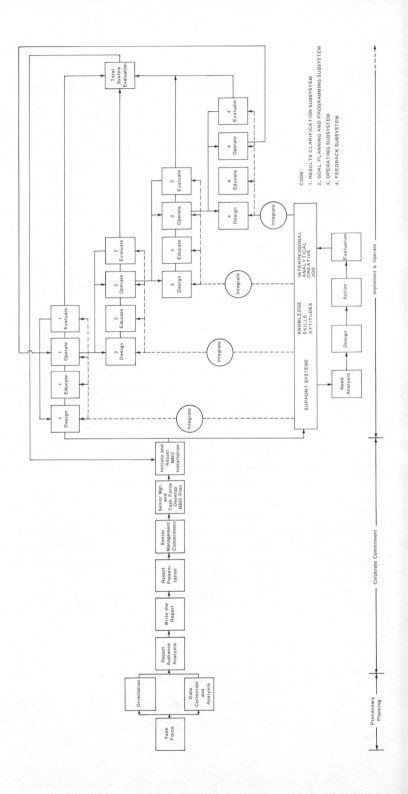

system for effectiveness and making the necessary revisions and improvements commensurate with experience.

Major departures from the original system are better handled by periodic educational meetings like those held when the system was first implemented. The quarterly progress review sessions also are an excellent, ongoing means for evaluating the system itself and making improvements.

Much of MBO is a state of mind—a way of doing things better and emphasizing continual improvement. Minds aren't changed overnight and neither will MBO become effective overnight.

Organizations that are considering adopting management by objectives and those that have already embraced it and are experiencing success on the low side of the scale would be well advised to examine critically the advantages and disadvantages of the three common approaches to implementation. For those still in the consideration stage, Figure 13 may help them avoid headaches later. For those who have moved beyond the consideration stage and are suffering the headaches already, Figure 13 may serve as a partial aspirin and help remove some of the ills.

Organizations can benefit from the experiences of almost every top manager who kicked off his MBO system with the "All Levels at Once" approach. When asked how their programs could have been improved and how they could have avoided many of the problems, invariably they answer that they should have followed the "One Level at a Time" means of implementation. Their reasons for now recommending the different approach are the disadvantages that are summarized in Figure 13 under the "All Levels at Once" method. In essence, the answers of these top people stress the desirability of devoting additional time to implementing MBO, proceeding in a gradual manner, and thoroughly digesting each bite before taking another one.

DISCUSSION CASE
Implementing MBO—the Manager's Dilemma

Mary Smith is the manager of office services of a large volunteer agency. She reports to the controller. The supervisors of the following units report to her: typing pool, mailroom, printing and reproduction, office supplies and equipment, and office custodial services.

Mary had attended a three-day session on management by objectives at one of the leading universities. Following this, she had done considerable reading on the subject and had discussed MBO with several of her acquaintances in other organizations who had experience with it. She decided she wanted to adopt MBO even though it would be new to her agency.

She met with her boss, briefed him on her knowledge of MBO, and informed him she would like to adopt it for her units for 1975. She received one of the following replies from the controller.

Alternative Answer A
The controller told Mary that MBO sounded like a lot of work and that he didn't want to get mixed up in such complicated crap.

Alternative Answer B
The controller commended Mary for her initiative and interest in exploring better ways of managing. Although he didn't know enough about MBO to adopt it throughout the controller's department, he encouraged her to proceed for her units. Possibly later, her experience could be used as the basis for other applications in the controller's department.

TEAM ASSIGNMENT

Assume that you are Mary Smith. Assume that you received Answer A. How would you go about convincing your boss that MBO would be a valuable asset to the management of your unit? Are there any parts of the system that you could implement on your own without going over your boss's head?

Assume that you received Answer B. Briefly outline how you would proceed to install MBO. Include the major parts of the system you would install. Indicate any problems you would have to consider.

11

case study

MBO in the Department of Health, Education, and Welfare

No book on MBO for nonprofit organizations would be complete without addressing itself to the application of MBO to the largest organization in the world. The U.S. Department of Health, Education, and Welfare—with a 1975 fiscal year budget of approximately $120 billion—ranks number one above all other organizations in both the nonprofit and business sectors. It dwarfs even such giants as the Department of Defense in the public sector and the American Telephone and Telegraph Company and General Motors in the private sector. Its annual budget is equal to about 8 percent of the gross national product of the United States as a whole in today's dollars.

Because of space limitations, this chapter will discuss only the "H" in HEW; namely, the Public Health Service (PHS). The "Ed-

Author's Comment: This chapter grew out of my experience as a consultant to HEW. It was prepared with the invaluable assistance of several of HEW's top administrators, who prefer not to be identified.

ucation" and "Welfare" components of the department are left to other authors and other times.

The Organization

Figure 15 is a simplified illustration of the organization of the Public Health Service. It is headed by the Assistant Secretary for Health (ASH), who reports directly to the Secretary of HEW. The PHS employs about 46,000 people and has a fiscal year budget of approximately $4.8 billion. Its operations cover the 50 states, the District of Columbia, Puerto Rico, the Virgin Islands, and the Pacific Trust Territories.

The two primary organizational entities of PHS that are most intimately involved in carrying out the MBO system are the regional offices and the health agencies. Each agency has responsibility for a broad area of the overall health field, and each agency is primarily responsible for program, policy, and budget development and evaluation in those areas for which it is responsible.

The majority of operations in the PHS are decentralized to ten regional offices, each headed by a regional health administrator (RHA). The regions are responsible primarily for operations and implementation of programs. The PHS regional office organization is represented in Figure 16. Operations of the ten regions are coordinated by the Office of Regional Operations (ORO), which is headquartered in Rockville, Maryland, and whose director reports directly to the Assistant Secretary.

This chapter will concern itself with the roles of the regional health administrators, agencies, and the Office of Regional Operations.

The MBO System

The PHS organization, represented in Figure 15, which was implemented in 1973, represents a significant reorganization of PHS regional operations. It involved a concerted effort to decentralize operations to the regional level and to permit the regional health administrators to play a more vital role in decision making and planning for their regions. Its ultimate aim is to improve management at the regional level and throughout the PHS.

Figure 15. Organization of the Department of Health, Education, and Welfare Public Health Service.

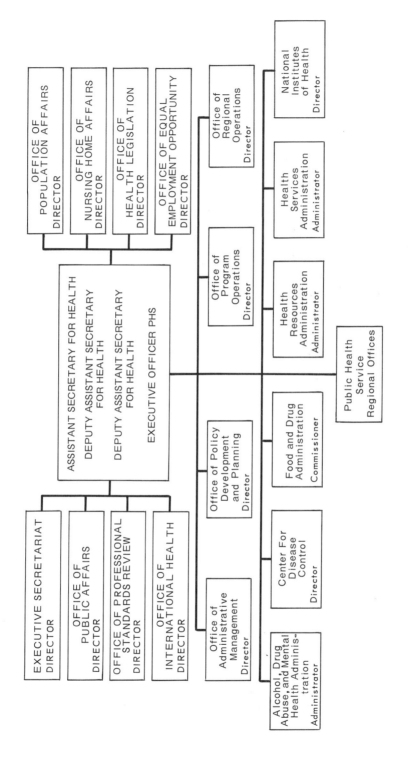

Figure 16. PHS regional office organization.

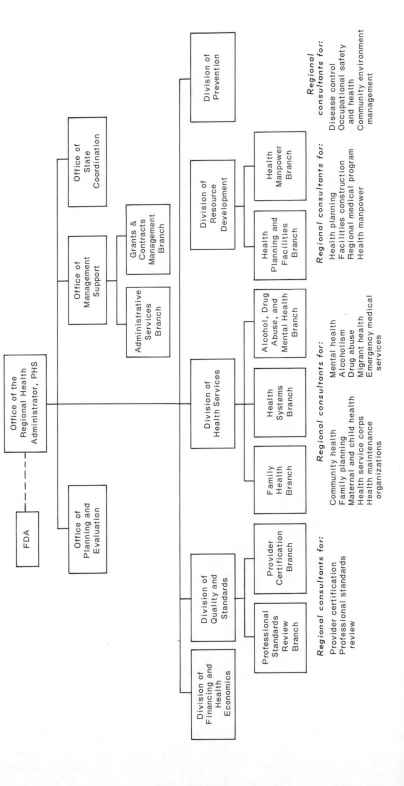

Following on the heels of the 1973 reorganization, PHS implemented what it refers to as its work planning system, or work program. (As is the case here, MBO frequently goes by different names.) The work planning system is described in the following paragraphs.

Work planning is a management tool that involves a systematic method of prioritizing and listing organizational objectives and plans, specifying the available financial and manpower resources that will be utilized to accomplish those objectives and establish a process of monitoring progress and providing feedback. The work program is the composite of all the RHA's objectives. The goal is to have this composite represent 100 percent of the financial and manpower resources for which the RHA is accountable. The work program is not restrictive or prescriptive but rather is supportive. The work program gives the RHA a base from which he can more effectively organize and manage the resources for which he is responsible.

The key elements of the work program planning process are the setting of results-centered objectives and targets, the development of detailed plans to support the objectives, the assignment of the resources necessary to carry out those plans, the identification of the manager responsible for carrying out specific objectives, and the identification of outputs relating objectives to specified needs and priorities including anticipated benefits and costs. After the RHA work program has been developed, there is reporting of current progress, the identification of problem areas, and the execution of management actions to counteract the effects of any problems.

The work program was developed in direct response to the charge by the Assistant Secretary for Health to the RHAs that they improve accountability for dollar and manpower resources. Thus the work program is a new way to operate in the regional offices and enables the RHAs to systematically plan and effectively manage their resources in order to achieve desired results and move toward insuring accountability.

The RHA's work program is designed to be a flexible, dynamic, developmental management tool that can be modified to further strengthen the management capabilities of the RHAs, to take advantage of the most current information available, and to accommodate changing policies and exigencies. Furthermore, it is designed to facilitate the interchange of information, provide a framework for assuring accountability, and maintain a cooperative and complementary relationship between the regional offices and the agencies.

Scope of Work Program and Specific Responsibilities

Key elements of the work program process are the setting of results-centered objectives and targets, the development of detailed plans, the assignment of the resources necessary to carry out those plans, the assignment of the objective manager, the monitoring of progress, the identification of problem areas, the execution of management actions to counteract the effects of any problems, and the provision of feedback.

The development and implementation process of the work program involves the following individuals and organizations. The RHA is responsible for the overall management of the work program process. The RHA determines regional office objectives and submits them to ORO and the agencies for negotiation and concurrence. For each objective, the RHA selects one person to be the objective manager with the authority and responsibility for its execution. The person to whom this responsibility is assigned estimates the resources needed for accomplishment, including personnel and funds, and so indicates upward to the RHA. If personnel assigned to other organizational entities are identified for the objective, their time is negotiated with the supervisor to whom they are assigned. The manager of the objective also negotiates with the RHA, or his designee, and reaches agreement with him on what is expected, when it is expected, and the resources available for accomplishment. Furthermore, the manager negotiates with all assignees to the objective with respect to their contribution and the indicators of successful performance.

The work program coordinator in each regional office has the responsibility for overall assistance and coordination of work program development, review, and monitoring of progress and performance. It is the responsibility of the assistant regional health administrator for management to insure that objectives and plans developed are consistent with available resources.

At the central office level, the health agencies set national priorities, communicate anticipated results, specify available resources, maintain programmatic and technical informational liaison with the regional program consultants, and negotiate with ORO and the RHAs concerning substance of the work program and required resources to be provided by the agencies to carry out regional objectives. The agencies designate an agency representative to assist in developing work programs that are consistent with and responsive to national program objectives. In addition, the agency administrators/directors attend the work program quarterly management conferences.

The Office of Regional Operations has the following responsibilities:

1. Develops, modifies, and maintains work program guidelines;
2. Coordinates development of planning guidance and updates as necessary;
3. Provides assistance in maintaining and improving the work program;
4. Arranges for regional office key staff to meet with agency key staff to provide regional office input into agency priorities as they are developed;
5. Concurs on regional plans;
6. Submits regional office work programs to agencies for review and concurrence; and
7. Assists PHS regional offices in negotiations with agencies.

Work Program Development

In addition to the continual programmatic and technical communication between the health agencies and the regional office program consultants, the health agencies and staff offices of PHS are requested to transmit to the RHAs, through ORO, national priorities, anticipated results, anticipated budget allocations (funds and positions), and proposed new initiatives by region. This information is formally communicated to the RHAs in a work program guidance document issued by ORO in February of each year. This information is continually updated through ORO during the budget/planning cycle.

Selection of Objectives

Selection should be responsive to priorities identified by:

1. Regional health administrators, directors of divisions and staff offices, and regional program consultants.

2. State and local health needs and resources.
3. Central office as identified by enacted legislation, Office of Manpower and Budget (OMB), secretary, agencies, and staff offices of PHS.
4. Regional directors.

For each objective, an overview and justification form is prepared as shown in Figure 17; the form should not be longer than two single-spaced typewritten pages. The overview and justification cite the statement of the objective and briefly state the rationale for selecting the specific objective. If possible and where applicable, the regional scope of the problem/activity being addressed by the objective is cited along with the regional scope of resources being directed to the problem/activity. The narrative also states the impact or result on the problem/activity that the objective is designed to achieve, the rationale behind the particular approach that has been selected to accomplish the objective, and the interrelationships of the objective to other objectives in the RHA work program.

The work plan accompanying the objective is shown in Figure 18. The resource delineation identifies all manpower and

Figure 17. Overview and justification form.

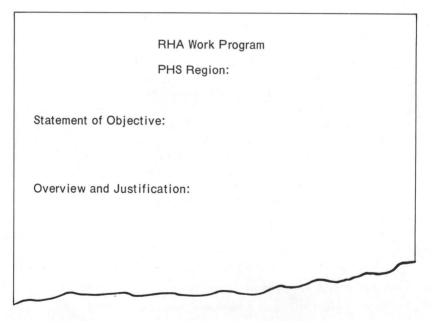

RHA Work Program

PHS Region:

Statement of Objective:

Overview and Justification:

Figure 18. RHA work program.

PHS Region: _____

Time Frame: _____

Objective Manager: _____

Organization Entity: _____

Objective Number: _____

Objective Statement: _____

Resources:	Central Office	Regional Office	Other	Total
Mondays (220/yr)				
Travel				
Contracts				
Project				
Formula				
Total				

Last date revised: _____

Central Office Action	Regional Action	Milestone & Action Step	Milestones (X = Action Steps)	Jul.	Aug.	Sep.	Oct.	Nov.	Dec.	Jan.	Feb.	Mar.	Apr.	May	Jun.

funds earmarked and approved for accomplishing the objective. In addition, the organizational entity or unit preparing the objective, the time frame for accomplishment, the date last revised, the manager responsible for achieving the objective, and the objective number are to be identified.

The columns for central office and regional offices can be used to indicate the person, organizational unit, or organization responsible for a particular action step.

The date last revised should always be changed whenever a substantial revision is made in a specific work plan.

Concurrence

The regional health administrator's work program draft is submitted to the Office of Regional Operations in May of each year for review and comment by PHS offices and agencies. ORO is responsible for distributing draft work programs, collecting comments, negotiating changes, and mediating differences between the RHAs and PHS offices and agencies. In addition, ORO reviews each work program on the basis of the following criteria:

Results-centered. The objective must state what results the objectives are designed to accomplish, what condition is desired to exist, or what impact the objective is expected to make.

Measurable. Objectives will be stated in terms of definite measures of achievement; that is, numbers of people to be served, numbers of projects to be initiated, or a clearly stated product.

Specificity. Objectives, work plans, and all supporting statements will be written in straightforward, unequivocal terms that leave no doubts in the mind of the reader as to just what is intended.

Feasibility. Objectives, work plans, and supporting statements will project work that can be accomplished, given appropriate management attention during the stated time frame. An objective must reflect policy decisions already made.

Timely. Objectives must be time-bounded.

The agencies and ORO provide final concurrence on each work program by the end of June.

Monitoring Work Program Process

The following monitoring guidelines are adhered to in order to insure that timely information will be available to meet the needs of the PHS, enhance the managerial capability and effectiveness of the RHA, and minimize the volume of paperwork.

Monthly management conferences are held between the RHA and his managers in order to track the progress on the RHA's objectives and plans. The RHA keeps a written record of the action items and their disposition resulting from the monthly management conferences.

Management conferences are held on a quarterly schedule with ASH, ORO, the agencies, and the RHAs to discuss in depth the status of the regional work program. Whenever possible, these meetings may be multiple-region reviews, which are held either in a regional office or in Parklawn. ORO provides a written summary and critique shortly after each conference to ASH, the RHAs and the agencies.

A written quarterly analysis and projection report is prepared for each RHA objective and plan. This report is prepared by the RHA's managers and submitted directly to the RHA. It is an internal document for use within the PHS regional office. The analysis and projection report contains the following elements: objective-identifying data, total resources required for accomplishment, accomplishments to date (completed action steps), percent of total resources expended to date, estimate for orderly completion of future milestones, brief statement of activities under way that would support this estimate, and recommendation for revision when problems are identified.

On an annual basis, the RHAs and ORO conduct an evaluation on the progress of the work program, analyzing its strengths and weaknesses and determining how it can be modified or improved to become a more effective management tool for the RHA. From time to time, ORO may request information regarding the status of specific objectives or resources.

Revision and Modification of Objectives or Plans

Significant revisions to RHA objectives and work plans must be submitted to ORO for concurrence. A significant revision would be one that would alter the scope and substance of the objective, critically affect the resource level, or extend the completion date for accomplishing the objective beyond a critical period. ORO will negotiate these changes with the agencies as a result of the RHA proposed revision. In addition, ORO will assist in procuring the necessary management assistance for the RHA to correct problems that may have necessitated the proposed revision.

Proposed revisions may be submitted to ORO for approval at any time. RHAs should not wait for the quarterly management conferences to propose their revisions. ORO will expedite the review of the proposed revision upon receipt and notify the RHA a short time thereafter as to its disposition.

Problems Encountered

Agencies were asked to present their priorities in measurable, results-centered objective statements to the regional offices. Certain agencies ostensibly encountered difficulty in responding to the request. What they presented as guidance was an array of activities or tasks to be performed. This type of guidance was of little value to the regions in developing their work programs consistent with MBO principles. It served to confuse the regions rather than to clarify what the regional roles would be in contributing to the achievement of a national objective. Much time and effort have been spent in trying to link the guidance tasks in some meaningful frame of reference in order to accomplish an objective in an RHA's work program. Activities are under way; for example, MBO training which will preclude the future occurrence of such guidance.

Here are some of the other major problems that were encountered.

1. One hundred percent of the resources were identified and tied to impact-oriented objectives. Although coverage of all activities and resources is conceptually viewed as necessary and desirable to a fully effective MBO process, the actual implementation created problems in a system that has traditionally focused management attention on selected priority and crisis issues. One problem was simply the practical implications of undertaking a planning process addressing all activities, many of which are considered routine and nonspecific, and for which the potential benefits of more focused management were felt not to be commensurate with the demands on already scarce management time and attention. A second problem is that planning to cover all activities implies an ability to plan for "unplanned" events. In the first year of implementation, this has posed considerable challenge in terms of how to provide for "contingencies," and how to reflect changing demands in a flexible, yet accountable system.

2. Follow-up training was not provided in certain regions. For various reasons, such as lack of time, enthusiasm, and tolerance for change, several regions chose not to pursue follow-up training. Although all the personnel concerned were familiar with basic concepts and terminology, moving into implementation without sufficient in-depth staff training appeared to result in:

Lack of flexibility. The focus was on complying with process rather than on creative adaptation to meet regional office needs.

Staff resistance. Operating staff, unfamiliar with the process, tended to participate reluctantly in implementation, viewing this solely as a top-down rather than an involved process.

Overreaction. Problems and complexities were easily exaggerated, and submissions tended to be overly detailed and voluminous.

3. Internal reorganization along functional lines occurred at the same time that the work program was being implemented. Although conceptually there appeared to be some benefit in consecutive implementation of the reorganization and the work program, this situation created perhaps the most significant single problem encountered in the first year of implementation. The functional reorganization and the work program process were both initiated to make changes to improve the management of regional offices—one dealing with structure, the second with process.

The primary problem posed was the effect on the employee morale of instituting very extensive and pervasive changes affecting the entire regional staff. Attempting to institute a new management process during a time of organizational uncertainty tended to heighten employee insecurity, dampen potential enthusiasm for aggressively pursuing the benefits of MBO, and, simply, added to the confusion of ill-defined working relationships. In some cases this situation served to exaggerate certain difficulties in implementing MBO. For example, how to reconcile the traditional flow of authority and responsibility along organizational lines with the process of management by objectives, which frequently crossed organizational lines.

Benefits

Some health agencies presented their national priorities as measurable, results-centered objectives to the regions in the work program guidance. In addition, they clearly identified the level of support needed in each regional office to accomplish the national objective. This approach enables each RHA to see what the big picture is with respect to a certain health issue and what the role of his region should be in contributing to the overall effort.

The implementation of the work program fostered team development in the regional offices. Generally, the achievement of an RHA objective, unless it is program-specific, requires an integrated effort from various program components, branches, divisions, or offices. For example, an RHA objective dealing with health-services funding would involve the efforts of the Division of Services as well as those of the Division of Financing and Health Economics. The team approach provides for the utilization of personnel with different skills to be used to achieve a common objective. The benefit is greater management flexibility in the regional office.

The RHA work program guidance of March 1, 1974, has proved to be a valuable PHS resource document. For the four PHS agencies with decentralized programs, the guidance provided (a) an overview of the agency's programs, citing its enabling legislation; (b) the program regulations either extant or under development; (c) a delineation of activities required to maintain program integrity in the regions; (d) identification of agency program priorities and areas of emphasis for fiscal year 1975; and (e) identification of regional expectations in support of agency objectives.

Never before had such a wealth of PHS programmatic information been displayed under one cover. This guidance was then followed by the RHAs to produce their work programs covering 100 percent of the resources available to the regions—another first.

The Future

Quarterly management conferences. The protocol for quarterly management conferences has been developed, and the Assistant Secretary for Health inaugurated the cycle with the first conference held in September 1974.

The conference will serve as a principal vehicle for providing feedback, monitoring progress, maintaining an interchange of management and programmatic ideas, surfacing problems, and identifying necessary corrective actions. It will be the forum in which the RHA will be prepared to respond to agency inquiries regarding progress on objectives and expenditure of resources as well as to identify problems that require agency attention. The agency heads will be prepared to respond to RHA inquiries regarding resources, agency policies, and support necessary to resolve issues and/or accomplish objectives.

Uniform work program guidance. A work group has been assembled to come to grips with the problem of providing uniform work program guidance. The work group comprised representatives from the regional offices, the agencies, and ORO. As a result of their efforts future agency work program guidance will:

1. Integrate agency priorities and anticipated resource levels.
2. Show a clear rationale for the resources allocated.
3. Highlight adjustments from one fiscal year to the next.
4. Provide in an overview section every aspect of a program prescribed by legislation.
5. Emphasize those elements of program guidelines that are high-priority for this fiscal year.
6. Provide a program overview for nonregionalized programs to serve as a resource document.
7. Provide agency and program objectives to the regions that are results-oriented.

Monitoring and feedback mechanisms. Each regional office has designed and implemented an internal monitoring and feedback system for its own work program. Each system varies considerably in its complexity and sophistication, from minimal reporting requirements in one region to an elaborate system complete with special forms in another. A monitoring and feedback mechanism designed by ORO personnel and a pilot region is being tested. The mechanism will provide feedback to the various levels of management, enabling (a) progress to be charted, (b) problems to be identified, (c) support and corrective action from the next higher echelon to be solicited and focused and (d) scarce management resources to be shifted to accomplish objectives that are in difficulty. Implementation of the mechanism will require a minimum of paperwork. If successful, the pilot will be employed, with slight modifications, in the other nine regions.

Training. Additional training courses will be provided to sharpen the MBO skills of the regional office personnel. Curriculum blocks will be developed dealing with the various elements of MBO as a system. The RHA will then select those blocks that he feels are most needed in his region to improve his work program. This approach will offer the advantage of tailoring the training to the specific needs of each region, while at the same time insuring uniformity in the training.

12

case study

MBO in the
Management Institute

Why are some educational service organizations successful while most are just average—and many are ineffective? In recent years, U.S. universities and colleges and their adjuncts have been subjected to heavy criticisms and pressures from legislatures, finance committees, trustees, students, parents, and taxpayers for a variety of reasons. In his most recent monumental volume, Peter Drucker insists that a major reason for the ineffectiveness of service organizations is the poor quality of *managerial performance*.[1]

As a long-time faculty member and management consultant, Drucker speaks with considerable authority on this subject. An or-

---

[1] Peter F. Drucker, *Management: Tasks, Responsibilities, Practices* (New York: Harper & Row, 1974).

Author's comment: Education is a major area of the nonprofit sector that is devoting increased attention to MBO. One of the older MBO installations has existed in the Management Institute of the University of Wisconsin since 1967. This chapter was contributed by Norman C. Allhiser, chairman of the Department of Business and Management, University of Wisconsin.

ganization that is completely dependent upon allocation from the budget, he says, frequently does not demonstrate effective performance results. Drucker suggests that performance in a service institution is the exception, rather than the rule, and that efficiency and cost control, however much they are preached, are not really considered virtues in the budget-based institution. Usually, the importance of a budget-based institution is measured by size of the budget and size of the staff. When an organization is budget-based, it makes it even more difficult to abandon wrong things; that is, the obsolete, the old. The typical response to lack of results is redoubling efforts to increase the budget, and/or blame the outside world.

Contrary to these dire observations, the Management Institute staff of the University of Wisconsin–Extension does not feel that it fits the above mold.

History of the Management Institute

The Management Institute (MI) is a section of the Department of Business and Management of the University of Wisconsin-Extension, located in Madison and Milwaukee. The Institute was founded in 1944 as an outgrowth of the World War II Engineering, Science, and Management War Training (ESMWT) program of the U.S. Office of Education. The Management Institute now employs a full-time staff of 15 faculty members, who in the past fiscal year conducted 350 programs (institutes, conferences, and seminars) for more than 11,000 management personnel.

The Institute is a professional education program service designed for practicing business and management personnel. MI has now been operating and growing for 30 years. It therefore is one of the oldest service institutions (and probably the largest) of its type in the world. During this period the Management Institute has evolved from a completely subsidized operation to a consistently high level of self-support. The approach has emphasized concern for the customer (the practical manager) and his needs and wants. The Institute has served more than 150,000 management personnel from all levels—first-line supervisor through organization president. The current annual budget now approximates $1 million. It offers programs in 12 different functional fields of management for some 3,500 firms and organizations throughout the United States and a number of foreign countries. These results didn't just happen. A dedicated professional staff made it happen.

The first Institute programs were designed to increase the supply of able supervisors for the war effort. The courses were categorized as training within industry and had titles like human relations training, methods improvement, and job instruction training. However, the growth of our economy, the continuing need for effective managers, and the support of the Wisconsin Manufacturers Association stimulated the early postwar expansion of the Institute offerings.

The following functional areas are now provided with management programming service: accounting and finance, administrative services, executive development, general management, industrial relations, manufacturing, marketing and sales, production and materials control, purchasing, supervision, training and development, and transportation.

Installing Management by Objectives

While it would make good copy to say that the management system used by the Institute was installed with deliberate foresight, objective analysis, and careful planning, that would be a misstatement. The process of managing with a systems approach gradually evolved—segmentally. To be more specific, my early concerns as a new administrator revolved around such considerations as improving faculty, institutional, and administrative performance.

Faculty members saw themselves primarily as instructors, not as administrators. Consequently, with loose administration, there were problems: missed deadlines of promotional brochures or incomplete information on bulletins, varying quality of programs, and differing competencies of resource leaders (guest instructors). Topics for programs were chosen on the basis of assumed needs, pure conjecture, or Ouija board methods.

One of the first approaches to resolving the performance problem was that of using position descriptions to identify and clarify faculty instructional and administrative responsibilities. There was considerable resistance to listing duties and responsibilities. The resistance revolved around the idea: "It's impossible to describe the work a professor does. The work is too complex. There are too many variables." The counterpoint was: "If one can't describe the work performed, how can one justify the activity involved as constituting a viable position?" A position description based on U.S. Employment Service occupational analysis concepts was eventually developed. After some early experimentation, it soon became apparent that while the job description explains *what* a person does in general terms, it does not provide a solution to the question, "How well is the individual performing his assignments?"

Consequently, the search continued to find a method that would provide viable feedback on performance effectiveness. The next efforts included the adoption of a merit-rating form, which listed 30 activities and personal qualities deemed essential to a good program coordinator. Some of the characteristics to be evaluated included loyalty, cooperation, appearance, friendliness, and ingenuity. Each characteristic was to be evaluated on a five-point scale from poor to excellent. The administrator's function was to rate each faculty member as he evaluated that professor's performance. These annual merit reviews could most charitably be described as a series of near disasters. Gradually it became evident that these sessions were destroying morale as well as a reasonably congenial administrative-staff relationship. The merit reviews failed—doomed from the start. There followed much soul-searching, many mental gymnastics, frequent attendance at personnel-oriented appraisal programs, and extensive reading in an effort to find solutions to the vexing performance problem.

Have you ever experienced a flash of insight after reading some new ideas? A chapter in Peter Drucker's *Practice of Management* provided the idea for the next step. The chapter was titled "Management by Objectives and Self-control." The implications of this insight from Drucker's concept forced a 180-degree turnaround in thinking about performance, work, and accomplishment. Drucker was not concerned about busyness or activities. He was interested in objectives and results. This concept made good common sense. Drucker said:

> The manager must know and understand what [business] goals demand of him in performance, and his superior must know what contribution to demand and expect of him, and must judge him accordingly.
>
> Each manager . . . needs clearly spelled-out objectives. These objectives should lay out what performance the man's own managerial unit is supposed to produce. They should lay out what contribution he is expected to make. . . . Finally, they [objectives] should spell out what contributions the manager can expect from other units,

toward the attainment of his own objectives. Right from the start, emphasis should be on team work and team results.[2]

The Implementation Process

After a number of abrasive staff meetings concerning the value of Drucker's ideas and the MBO approach, the decision was made to investigate, to explore, and eventually to pilot the approach. At that point, there were no how-to manuals. No step-by-step procedures had been set down. The management guide formulated by Standard Oil of California and Ed Schleh's classic book, *Management by Results*, proved to be helpful.[3] Schleh emphasized such key concepts as these: In working with subordinates one must make it a full job and delegate by results. Furthermore, accountability must be personal; planning responsibilities must be broadened; individuals must have the freedom to act, and even have freedom to make mistakes.

He also insisted that sound supervisory practice required adherence to the following principles:

Set up objectives.
Train and develop men.
Check on progress.
Stimulate through follow-up.
Call personnel to account.

Guidelines for Staff Performance

The first segment of the MBO system to emerge and succeed to some degree was an identification and clarification of functions or key performance areas. This segment became known as guidelines for staff performance. The guidelines consisted of objectives and standards that had been quantified and/or qualified to serve as a basis for performance expectation, measurement, and evaluation. With active staff involvement, functions of faculty members were identified and agreed upon. Key performance results areas were identified as (a) programming, (b) administration, (c) self-development, (d) instruction, (e) contributions, and (f) services.

As an example of how an objective emerged, there was some

[2] *The Practice of Management* (New York: Harper & Row, 1954), pp. 121–136.
[3] New York: McGraw-Hill, 1961, pp. 75–87.

concern about the quality of instruction because quality varied considerably with different staff members and different ad hoc instructors. Improving instructional quality subsequently became a key results area. Early on, it was determined that more emphasis must be placed on the needs and wants of the "consumer," the participant–user. Initially, in postmeeting checklists, participants were asked to react to about 15 items relating to the leader's presentation, methods, personality, knowledge, and his general effectiveness. This approach proved to be time-consuming and cumbersome. There was a need to quantify participant responses and establish some type of par. The following simplified procedure emerged.

Resource leaders would be rated on the basis of (1) the session as a whole, (2) benefits, and (3) leadership. For each element there would be five possible gradations: excellent, very good, good, fair, and poor. Figure 19 illustrates the evaluation form. All participant reactions for a given session would be combined to secure a *total* group response for each of the three elements. This rating would constitute the total participant reaction to the specific session.

Figure 19. Resources leader evaluation form.

SESSION REACTIONS FOR _____ PROGRAM

Subject _____ Leader _____

1. How would you rate this session?
    Excellent ____ ; Very good ____ ; Good ____ ; Fair ____ ; Poor ____ .

2. Were there portions of the subject matter that could have been excluded or expanded?
    _____
    _____
    _____

3. Do you feel you benefited from this session?
    Very much so __ ; Generally, yes __ ; To some extent __ ; Slightly __ ; No __ .
    If so, how? _____

4. What is your overall rating of the leader?
    Excellent ____ ; Very good ____ ; Good ____ ; Fair ____ ; Poor ____ .
    Please comment on your rating: _____
    _____
    _____
    _____

How did one know when the instructor achieved a par rating? After considerable discussion it was determined that a rating of 3.7 should be established as a desirable objective, or par, for each instructor's presentation. This objective was built into the guidelines for staff performance, and now serves a number of purposes:

1. To provide the faculty member with immediate feedback on participants' reactions.
2. To provide some guidance for the program administrator in coaching an ad hoc discussion leader.
3. To become *one* tangible session result that could be added to each faculty member's total number of fiscal year teaching assignments for measurement against his annual instructional objective.

To illustrate, the faculty member would establish an objective at the beginning of the fiscal year: "To teach 50 management sessions during the fiscal year and attain an overall rating of 3.7." Here, then, are a number of critical elements that have been built into the process of using the objective as a tool:

1. Identification of a key result area (quality of program).
2. Quantified measurement (50 sessions, 3.7, fiscal year [time]).
3. A process for measuring (cumulative, instruction, records).
4. Immediate feedback of result (reaction sheets).
5. A procedure for evaluation against objective.

Although this participant reaction sheet is a long way from perfect, it has proved to be a very valuable tool for self-evaluation, adjustment in teaching approach, and guidance for coaching.

Building the Segments into a System

It soon became clear that an effective approach to management required more than job descriptions, merit ratings, and guidelines for staff performance. Although each segment served an important function, individual segments did not forge the section into a truly cohesive unit. To point up the approach taken in formulating the system, we can apply some lessons learned from successful teams in the sports field. More specifically, teamwork can be illustrated with a well-managed football organization. A successful team gets the best results (touchdowns) when:

All members know the *purpose.*
All agree on the *objectives.*
Each member is *fully trained* and is at peak performance.
Strategic plans are properly implemented.
Plays are correctly timed and *coordinated.*
Team plays and individual performances are *evaluated.*
Continuing individual- and team-play *improvements* are made.

Likewise, a service organization can utilize a system to develop better teamwork. Why does a good system work better? It works much better than any other approach because all members of the staff have been involved in its development, and are committed to essential agreement on:

Our mission (purpose).
Objectives—unit and individual. (Accountabilities are accepted and understood.)
Strategic plans—priorities for concentration.
Programs developed and implemented.
Integrated effort.
Periodic evaluation and feedback.
Performance improvement.

In this type of organization, there are continuing opportunities for achievement, learning and growth, and self-actualization as well as tangible recognition and consequent self-esteem. These individual satisfactions are invaluable motivational byproducts of the system.

The Mission

What is our mission? Our purpose? Our reason for being? These basic questions occupied a good share of our time and energy. The early mission statements were somewhat crude and lacked clarity of intent, possibly because there was no clear guidance available on how to write a mission. For example, one statement read: "To build the best industrial management development program in the United States." We learned that a mission defined the "nature of the work to be performed." Further, we learned that such statements could normally include elements involving functional commitment, support determination, broadness of scope, uniqueness of contributions, and market and geographical considerations.

The mission statement should serve as a solid base for the unit's management system for a number of reasons: (1) It serves as a source for establishing objectives; (2) it provides a means for determining the validity of objectives; (3) it establishes accountability for ultimate results. With these general guidelines in mind, the mission statements have been reviewed every other year. Currently, the mission statement reads: "The programming mission of the Management Institute shall be to provide daytime management development short courses for managers, administrators, and professionals in business and service organizations." Our client group has become worldwide; hence no geographical barriers are included in the statement. Whereas we were once serving largely manufacturing and industrial groups, we now have management personnel from many profit and nonprofit service organizations as well. That accounts for the changes in our mission statement.

The Management Institute divisional mission now ties into our broader Department of Business and Management mission, which reads: "To provide continuing education to meet the needs of managers and professionals in industry, business, and government." Historically, securing agreement on the mission statement has been a real challenge. Staff members have probably had more protracted arguments over this segment of the system than any other before coming to mutually agreeable views on purpose. The above mission statements are definitely not the final word. There must be continuing review and periodic adjustment to the dynamics of adult management education.

Now it became increasingly clear that the mission and functions of the organization were rather closely related. Therefore, the function and the mission must be linked in the system. While the mission was being developed, the sectional functions were further defined and clarified as a part of the process. Again, there was considerable discussion before reaching agreement on the role and function of the Management Institute. Eventually, nine functions were established. They were:

1. Programming
2. Innovation
3. Marketing
4. Climate
5. Administration

6. Service
7. Staffing
8. Public relations
9. Finance

There was now general agreement on our reason for existence and the work we had to perform. So another major element was built into the management system.

Organizational Objectives

The next task was to establish organizational objectives. Marvin Bower in his excellent book *The Will to Manage* states, "Managing is the task of determining the objectives of the organization and then guiding the people and other resources of the organization in the successful achievement of these objectives." [4] Establishing objectives then became the next segment to be built into the system. Developing objectives to determine what results we wished to accomplish proved to be one of the most difficult and critical parts of the process. Again, it was essential to review the mission and the major functions and to try to identify the key result areas for the various functions. Admittedly the quality of the first objectives left much to be desired. In fact, it is doubtful whether they met many of the criteria currently considered essential: Objectives should be measurable, challenging, attainable, specific, and integrated with organizational goals.

Objectives were subsequently modified, added, and discarded in the annual planning and postreview sessions. Objectives are still not perfect tools for management, but they have served a number of useful purposes. They have improved direction for operational activities, provided guides for priorities of staff emphasis, encouraged better functional and organizational planning, served as a vehicle for faculty self-measurement of progress, assured a rational evaluation of performance, and established a fairer base for work appraisal.

Establishing Objectives

Initially, there was a strong tendency on the part of the director to arbitrarily impose objectives in the areas of finance (100 per-

[4] New York: McGraw-Hill, 1966.

cent self-support), programming quality (3.8 out of 4.0), and size of individual workload (20 programs annually). Outright opposition developed, so the approach had to be changed. Increasingly, it became obvious that to secure staff support and cooperation, faculty had to be involved and committed to the objectives. A compromise was reached that provided for high attainment as well as maximum staff involvement in the objective-setting process. Each functional program administrator would first develop his own objectives in conjunction with the director for that particular functional area. Then all objectives for individual functional units would be combined. The combined functional objectives would then become organizational objectives for the Institute. In general that approach has worked reasonably well. Some typical objectives follow.

General and Continuing Objectives

1. To help improve performance of clients in their present positions.
2. To help prepare selected management personnel for greater responsibility.
3. To provide educational opportunities to broaden the knowledge and understanding of technical and specialized management personnel.

Specific Annual Objectives

1. To conduct 350 programs in *ten* functional areas of management.
2. To attain a quality rating of 3.7 (on a scale of 4.0) for 790 days of programming offered in Madison and Milwaukee.
3. To achieve 20 *percent* innovation in programming.
4. To teach 564 instructional sessions with a quality rating of 3.7 by 15 staff members.
5. To reach an enrollment goal of 10,000 participants.
6. To maintain a high level (90 *percent* or better) of self-support.
7. To encourage continuing learning and growth opportunities for staff members.

Thus a hierarchy of objectives evolved for the organization. Each staff member developed his own objectives with his supervisor.

Figure 20. Work plan and achievement report.

			From:		To:	
Last Name	First			(Six-Month Period Covered)		

Department of Business and Management

I. COORDINATION

A. Institutes

Goals	Program Days			Enrollment	Program Rating
	Total	New	Repeat		

Actual Totals	Program Days			Enr.	# Canc.	Program Rating
	Total	New	Repeat			

Two-to five-day programs. List all programs scheduled.

Date	Title	Program Days			Enrollment		Canc.	Program Rating
		T	N	R	Plan	Act.		

Supervisors developed objectives for the functional area they administered. The combined functional objectives of the ten units constituted the base for the Institute objectives. To date we have not found a better approach for this faculty-oriented, democratically operated method. The third segment had now been built into the management system.

The vital importance of mission, situation analysis strategies, and objectives as part of the planning process in management thus acknowledged, it became increasingly apparent that some type of "plan for planning" was essential to integrate the various elements of the planning procedure. Such a plan would have to include provision for internal communications and budgeting. Consequently, a plan for planning was developed for the guidance of each individual staff member and program director, as well as for overall Institute operations. The planning process included three stages: first, individual planning by each staff member; second, section planning by each program director; third, overall Institute planning by the director and committees.

Individual Objectives

While primary attention was given to annual planning considerations, biennial budgeting and programming also forced simultaneous emphasis on two- to three-year or longer-range projections. The process then started with individual planning. Each staff member was encouraged to develop a plan of work. The purpose of this plan was to have faculty members plan, organize, schedule, staff, and budget work 12 to 15 months in advance of each upcoming fiscal year. As a part of this plan, the staff person was to establish his specific objectives for the fiscal year. Normally these objectives cover such critical areas as programs, program schedules, innovation, ratings, instructional sessions, and enrollments. Specific plans for professional growth are strongly emphasized. The work plan thus serves as a guide for faculty members for the entire year. During the course of the fiscal year the plan is also used three times as a basis for progress review discussions on the member's objectives, plans, problems, accomplishments, and updating of adjustments on elements of the plan (Figure 20). Individual planning of workload tended to follow the procedure outlined below.

*Planning Workloads (Individual Faculty
Member Responsibilities)*

1. Develop individual workload plan.
2. Present individual objectives and plans to functional administrator in the applicable areas of:
   (a) Programming
   (b) Instruction
   (c) Research

(d) Publication
(e) University service
(f) Professional service
(g) Public service
(h) Consulting
(i) Self-development

3. Reach mutual agreement with administrator on plans.
4. Arrange for implementation of all objectives.
5. Meet with administrator periodically to review progress on objectives.
6. Prepare a personal achievement report by July 1, reviewing accomplishments during preceding year.
7. Discuss with immediate supervisor:
    (a) Achievements
    (b) Problems from past year
    (c) Plans for next year
8. Base *new* plans on results of conference (in writing), and future programming, instruction, research, publications, and the like as in No. 2 above.

Plans are then consolidated for each section. Section plans serve as critical inputs for the situation analysis. Total results are tabulated, analyzed, and interpreted in the situation analysis for number of programs, number of program days, new programs—innovations, instructional sessions, evaluations, income and expense, enrollments, as well as economic trends, political developments, sociological considerations, and market analysis.

The results thus obtained are translated into objectives or standards for the next fiscal year. New objectives resulting from a situation analysis indicating potential opportunities, new strategies, or probable problem areas are formulated. Each section is now in a position to establish a sound basis for its own master plan.

The Total Plan

For the past few years, a master plan has been developed for the entire Institute operation. The master plan focuses on critical internal as well as external factors and consists of the following elements:

A mission statement
Current policies
Objectives
  Long-range
  Short-range
Plans
  Institute
  Sectional
  Individual
Budget
  Annual
  Biennial
Implementation of plans
  Programs
  Arrangements
  Facilities
  Promotion
Controls and evaluation
  Periodic financial reports (monthly)
  Enrollment reports (weekly)
  Reaction sheets (each session and each program)
  Performance reviews (three times per year)
  Annual reviews

Policy Guidelines

Over a period of time, policy guidelines have been developed to further refine the system. For example, programming was identified as the single most critical area of our operation. Indeed, although it truly represented only one of our functions, it did account for 80 percent of our total effectiveness as an organization. Hence the following guidelines emerged on programming:

1. Stress high-quality programming and instruction at every level in every functional area.
2. Emphasize practical, realistic approach to meeting management needs, solving problems, and achieving goals in formulating programs.
3. Employ functional specialists in each programming area— with a combination of business and academic experience.
4. Develop strong relationship with functional advisory com-

mittees to secure continuing input and evaluation on programs.

5. Insure that evaluation is an inherent part of the programming improvement process.

To illustrate point 5: Just as reaction sheets were used to evaluate speakers, it soon became clear that such evaluations could also be applied to programs. Reaction sheets are now employed to obtain the participants' comments at the conclusion of each program. Program reaction sheets permit the user to give his opinions about the entire Institute, conference, or seminar. The program objective is computed in the same manner as the individual instructional session. The program objective is 3.7, or in some sections 3.8. Cumulative records are maintained for each program for each staff member on all programs he coordinates.

Early management guidelines that evolved could be categorized as follows:

1. There would be professional administration of all facets of operations—planning, organizing, staffing, promoting, and conducting programs.
2. A master plan would be developed to include programs, budget, schedules, arrangements, and facilities.
3. All planning—for unit, sections, and individuals—would be tied into master plan.
4. Annual progress review would be conducted with and by each unit head.
5. Evaluation and continual upgrading of speakers and programs would be built into the system.
6. A climate for dedicated faculty members and administration would be fostered with maximum personal freedom and independence of functional operations.

In addition, policy guidelines were formulated on faculty and ad hoc staffing. Some typical guidelines follow.

1. Extreme care should be exercised in the selection and coaching of ad hoc resource leaders.
2. Work toward the right mix of academic, practitioner, and consultative personnel in staffing.
3. Provide opportunity for faculty and staff to take advantage of outside work and consulting assignments for continued learning and growth.
4. Develop self-improvement and personal growth plans.

Thus from a strictly seat-of-the-pants approach to operating by activity, this service organization has moved through a variety of learning experiences. This evolutionary process has resulted in a more professional approach to management. In effect, we agree with Drucker:

> What service organizations need is not better people. They need people who do the management job systematically and who focus themselves and their institution purposefully on performance and results. They do need efficiency, that is, control of costs, but above all they need effectiveness, that is, emphasis on the right results.[5]

Our system, which is composed of a mission, policies, objectives, plans, procedures, budgets, evaluation, and feedback, is the result of faculty participation and involvement, with a strong commitment to continued improvement of programming, instruction, and administration. We are convinced that effective performance in a service organization is entirely feasible—provided the system is properly designed, adapted, and implemented.

[5] Op. cit., p. 66.

13

case study

Management
by Agreement
at Hartford Hospital

In February 1968, I submitted a recommendation to the administrator of Hartford Hospital entitled "The Improvement of Managerial Effectiveness." In this memorandum I contrasted the managerial effectiveness of the three organizations I had been associated with over a 15-year period—Company A, Company B, and Hartford Hospital. It was my belief that Company A did a consistently superior job in the planning function at all organizational levels and that this approach enabled the company to remain a leader in its field. On the other hand, Company B did not give planning the emphasis it deserved, which resulted in many serious problems for the company. I felt that Hartford Hospital fell somewhere between these two extremes since certain kinds of planning received major and appropriate emphasis, such as planning for new facilities, but that individual managerial planning and goal setting were being carried out only in a small number of departments. I did

Author's comment: Hospitals are rapidly adopting management by objectives. I am grateful to Robert C. Gronbach, assistant administrator of Hartford Hospital (Hartford, Connecticut), for describing the experience of his hospital.

believe that managerial effectiveness at Hartford Hospital was of a high order because of the caliber of the people in key positions. However, I also felt that certain improvements could be made, particularly in the area of goal setting by individual managers. Here is how I viewed Hartford Hospital's major problems at the time:

PROBLEM   PROPOSED SOLUTION

Planning

The objectives of various departments of Hartford Hospital need to be better coordinated with overall hospital objectives. This problem exists partly because of mixed allegiances due to professionalism and partly because of inadequate communication on this subject.

A new approach to management that emphasizes the setting of objectives by department heads and supervisors and the coordination of these objectives with hospital objectives. This is the so-called management by objectives or goal-setting approach to management.

Organizing

We have a rigidity in organization structure in certain areas. Change is not occurring quickly enough to meet new demands brought on by increasing hospital size and complexity.

The organization planning committee is examining some of these problems and will make recommendations on this subject in this calendar year. Other groups are also working on many of these problems.

Directing

We want to improve the capability of everyone in a managerial position to stimulate employees to move effectively toward hospital goals.

Let's step up efforts in management and supervisory development. The addition of a training director has enabled us to move toward improvement in these areas. Much more needs to be done.

Controlling

One problem has been to provide department heads and supervisors with sufficient feedback regarding their departments so that resources can be better controlled. A second problem is to improve our managerial appraisal system.

The new annual budgeting system with frequent feedback to department heads will be of considerable assistance in improving the controlling function, particularly if integrated with a management by objectives approach.

All the solutions indicated here, including the Hartford Hospital approach to management by objectives, were implemented within six years.

Special Considerations

In considering the implementation of a management by objectives program in a hospital, it is important to take into consideration the unique characteristics and special problems of a nonprofit hospital. (Hartford Hospital has close to 1,000 beds and the equivalent of 3,000 employees.)

1. A nonprofit hospital usually has a medical staff relating to it, with considerable influence over hospital goals, priorities, and budgets, without being directly accountable for results. One can imagine the difficulty involved in gaining acceptance of a management by objectives approach by a private physician who is not an employee of the hospital.

2. Partly because of the presence of the medical staff, most hospitals have adopted an approach to management that emphasizes decision making by committee. There are usually a number of administrative and medical committees devoted to discussion, review, and decision making in many aspects of the hospital's functioning. Such a situation adds to the difficulties of applying a management by objectives system, which is essentially based on a one-to-one relationship. It is difficult for one person to have objectives and to be held accountable for results that have become the responsibility of a committee.

3. Hospitals, particularly large medical centers, are much more complex than many industrial organizations, continuing medical and nursing services and such functions as a large hotel, a busy restaurant, emergency room services, social services, the equivalent of a college and a vocational school, as well as all the usual functions of management found in industry. This degree of complexity makes for increased difficulty in coordinating goals and setting priorities.

4. Hospital planning, budgeting, and rate setting must be reviewed by a variety of government agencies. A hospital administrator and a board of directors may no longer make major decisions without a variety of government approvals. This hinders decision making and goal setting by those who continue to be held accountable for results.

The Approach

Considering these unique characteristics, I proposed an approach to management by objectives that I identified as management by agreement—a designation that more accurately describes the emphasis our program places on mutual agreement by the supervisor and the subordinate at each step in the management by objectives process. The program was proposed to be voluntary, with each manager deciding whether or not he wished to apply the program in his department. Training and coaching would be emphasized, and the program would be offered to all managerial, executive, and professional personnel. It was decided not to require all members to utilize this approach because we agreed with Douglas McGregor's view. He felt that a manager could not be coerced into managing in a style foreign to his natural tendencies or conditioning. Therefore, our job was to develop managers to the point where they would willingly adopt management by agreement.

The proposal was accepted as hospital policy, and the implementation began in 1968. Our first step was to clarify overall hospital objectives. Obviously, a manager cannot set clear objectives unless he knows, and agrees with, and is clear regarding overall goals. Clarification of overall objectives was accomplished through a participative process that involved input from hospital administration, the medical staff, department heads, supervisors, and employees. The overall objectives of the hospital were:

> To provide the community with efficient, high-quality health care and to cooperate with other health agencies toward this end.
>
> To encourage and support comprehensive educational programs that will supply the community with the skilled personnel necessary to provide efficient, high-quality health care.
>
> To encourage and support medical and administrative research programs that will result in improvements in health care.
>
> To plan and provide for continuing growth and change to meet the health needs of a growing, changing community.
>
> To enable employees to achieve personal goals through the achievement of hospital objectives.

With overall goals clarified, the next step was to publicize the new program, conduct general sessions to explain the program, distribute explanatory booklets, and schedule the necessary seminars. The following is a summary of the management by agreement procedure. Figure 21 illustrates the procedure graphically.

Figure 21. Management by agreement procedure.

Procedure

The individual manager's responsibilities are clarified, goals for the coming year are agreed upon, and an appraisal takes place at the end of the year on the basis of previously agreed upon goals. This procedure differs from some management by objectives programs in that it emphasizes the reaching of agreement at each step in the procedure.

Step 1: Clarification

The manager's job duties, responsibilities, and authority levels are clarified by first having the individual complete a job description. The manager then discusses the conditions of his job with the supervisor, and agreement is reached regarding duties, responsibilities, and authority levels. The next step should not be taken until both parties have clarified the job in this way and general agreement is reached.

Step 2: Goal Setting

The manager is asked to establish specific performance goals for the coming 12-month period. Goals should be well defined, realistic, as measurable as possible, and scheduled. They should include both work goals and individual development goals (see Figure 22).

The manager then discusses his goals with the supervisor, and agreement is reached on a final listing of goals and their priority. Wherever possible, completion dates are recorded. Throughout

Figure 22. Completed management by agreement form.

Complete in duplicate and return one copy to your chief, department head, or management member prior to the goal-setting discussion.

Name: Ronald Jones   Department: Personnel
Position: Director   Date: Sept. 28, 197___

Accomplishments during the past year. List goals achieved or steps completed in the achievement of uncompleted goals.

1. Promoted to position of personnel director.
2. Became familiar with people and many of the procedures and policies in the personnel department.
3. Became a member of Connecticut Personnel Association, Connecticut Hospital Personnel Directors Association, American Society of Hospital Personnel Association, Greater Hartford Chamber of Commerce Employers Committee.
4. Organized and presented a successful New England Hospital Association seminar, "How to Control Sick Time."
5. Recommended and installed a general salary adjustment.
6. Helped orient new director of food service.
7. Helped resolve difficulties with new parking system.
8. Set up a monthly in-service education program for personnel assistants.

List your most important goals for the coming year, including self-development goals. Be specific, as these items will be the basis for a discussion with your chief, department head, or management member. This information will be the basis for the joint establishment of goals.

1. Accomplish reunion of personnel department in Bliss One.
2. Examine procedures, methods, systems of the personnel department to eliminate or streamline those that are outdated or seldom used. Begin after move.
3. Review and realign clerical and secretarial workloads, with the goal of eliminating 20 hours of clerical help. Define and consider impact of TSA and LTD. Begin after move.
4. Provide cross-training within personnel so that at least two people know each special assignment. Begin now.
5. Provide cross-training of personnel assistants in other departments through work assignments. Begin after Bliss Wing and start of No. 4.
6. Develop personal skills through attendance in appropriate seminars in (a) wage and salary administration, (b) labor relations, (c) job evaluation. To be accomplished as appropriate courses are offered through AMA, AHA, and the like.
7. Develop a better "sign on" procedure. Begin now, finish December 197___.
8. Develop a videotaped orientation program and evaluate. Start now.
9. Work with security team to improve control and policing of parking garage and lot.

This side of form to be completed during the goal-setting discussion.

The goal-setting discussion is to center on the goals outlined on the opposite side of this form. After you and your chief, department head, or management member come to *agreement* on these goals and their priorities, list them in the space below. Be specific in listing target dates and concrete actions to be taken.

1. Examine the short- and long-term impact of the School of Nursing on staffing and recruitment procedures with appropriate recommendations to be made (June 15, 197____).

2. Work with community agencies on programs that contribute to community well-being and hospital goals to be accomplished through the year, with an emphasis on the Urban League and the Community Renewal Team.

3. To move and consolidate personnel department into new quarters and to examine and reorganize work assignments, office procedures, and systems, reviewing the possibility of reducing the staff by one half-time clerk, to be accomplished by July 31, 197____.

4. To develop personnel skills through attendance at seminars in (a) wage and salary administration (June 197____) and (b) labor relations, American Hospital Association seminar, in August 197____.

5. Work with the security department to improve the control and policing of parking garage and lots, establishing a system for tagging cars without stickers by November 197____, and to increase surveillance in parking areas to reduce or eliminate car thefts.

6. Provide cross-training within the personnel department so that at least two personnel assistants are knowledgeable of all special assignments, with job rotation to take place throughout the year.

7. To develop a videotape orientation program, with the script to be accomplished by December 197____.

Keep a copy of this form for your reference. The original will be placed in your confidential personnel folder located in the office of the director of employee relations.

To be completed by chief, department head, or management member:

The accomplishments of this individual during the past year contributed toward the goals of Hartford Hospital as follows (check one category):

_____ Very superior contribution
_____ Superior contribution
_____ Satisfactory contribution
_____ Less than satisfactory contribution
_____ Little or no contribution

Date of goal-setting discussion:

Signature of employee _____   Signature of _____
                                         chief, department head, or management
                                         member

Signature of executive director or designate _____

the year, additional sessions will be held to review progress, adjust priorities, and change goals as conditions may dictate.

Step 3: Appraisal

At the end of the year, the individual appraises his or her own performance by comparing results with goals previously set. This is done in writing. The self-appraisal is then discussed with the supervisor, and agreement is reached regarding the individual's performance during the previous 12-month period. This may then lead to salary action, if appropriate, which is communicated to the employee in a separate interview. We believe that the salary review interview should be separated from the performance review session to prevent the manager from concentrating solely on salary matters rather than performance as measured against goals.

As can be seen, this program focuses on motivation and development in its emphasis on reaching agreement, stresses the importance of flexibility in goal setting over the year, and underlines the importance of concluding the procedure with performance appraisal. Recently, I heard someone say that personnel specialists have ruined MBO by turning it into an appraisal tool. Obviously, I disagree with this view. When one provides a salary increase to a subordinate on the basis of performance, the most significant aspects of that individual's performance will be the accomplishment or lack of accomplishment of goals previously set. In my opinion, it is not possible to divorce appraisal from MBO.

Experience to Date

Recently, we conducted a survey to determine the MBO training needs of Hartford Hospital personnel. Seventy-two percent of the personnel included in the program felt the need for additional training. Respondents were also asked what advantages they found in using the management by agreement process. The following reasons were given, and are listed in order of frequency:

1. Provides a better opportunity to analyze and evaluate performance through discussion.
2. Provides an opportunity to evaluate past performance and allows for agreement on future goals.
3. With definite written goals, an employee knows what he

should be accomplishing and has a greater sense of commitment.

4. Goals are clearly defined and the system is good; however, application varies with supervisors.
5. The system is more objective and is beneficial to development.

The respondents also provided the following disadvantages of management by agreement, which are listed in order of frequency:

1. Very time-consuming. However, some felt that this factor is a necessary evil.
2. Situation and priorities change rapidly, so that previously set goals are no longer pertinent.
3. The system becomes repetitive because of the inflexible structure of some jobs.
4. Setting goals for one year is too restrictive for some jobs.
5. Goals are often hard to state in writing.

An analysis of these survey responses indicates that we have not as yet reached the promised land. Obviously, more training is needed and we intend to provide it. More effort is needed to encourage both private and salaried physicians to take part in management by agreement. Committee goal setting needs to be integrated more with individual goal setting. We need to do a better job of integrating the annual budgeting process with individual goal setting. At present, the budgeting process precedes, and with government approval sets the parameters for, individual goal setting. What is needed is a more integrated approach where both the budgeting process and the management by agreement process influence each other concurrently, so that both the annual budget and departmental and individual goals are developed and accomplished together over the same time span.

To summarize, I would say that over a six-year period we have made a fair degree of progress in implementing our approach to management by objectives. Virtually all our middle- and top-level managers utilize the program. We are presently attempting to include more salaried physicians in the program where some resistance to the concept continues. Many department heads testify as to the value of the program both in clarifying their goals and in helping to coordinate their department goals with the goals of other departments. This is in addition to indicating that the program provides a very effective appraisal method. As to the overall impact on the hospital, it is my judgment that there has been considerable impact on the functioning of various hospital departments, but a significant overall impact will be made when our program evolves into a systems approach that integrates budgeting, top-level planning, and management by agreement. It is my personal objective to help the hospital continue to move in this direction.

14

case study

Lutheran Social Services of Wisconsin and Upper Michigan

Historically, social welfare has directed its attention to two major classes of individual, family, and community problems—income deficiencies and personal and family disturbance and disorganization. Private and government agencies have addressed these problems with a variety of income-maintenance and social-work-service approaches. Since the 1930s social welfare legislation has given government a virtual monopoly in the provision of income through public assistance (relief) and social insurance (Social Security) programs. Growth in government services was rapidly accelerated with "Great Society" legislation in the 1960s.

Private social agencies, excluded from income-maintenance programs by overwhelming need and limited resources, moved to

Author's comment: One of the more challenging areas for the managing and ordering of priorities is the field of social services. I am grateful to Rev. Benjamin A. Gjenvick, executive director of Lutheran Social Services, for contributing the contents of this chapter.

further develop social-work services in relation to family and individual adult and child problems. Intensive, large-scale efforts were made in professional schools of social work and in social agencies to create professional helping techniques that would effectively address complex human needs and problems.

Progress in the development and application of management techniques lagged in both the government and private sectors. The declining proportion of total services provided by private agencies was either insufficiently recognized or inadequately addressed. The fact that social services are a public necessity and that they cannot be made generally available with contributed funding is only now gaining recognition in the private field. (The wide acceptance of a socialist bias in social welfare in favor of government services has contributed to this situation.)

Management excellence has been further inhibited by so-called deficit financing by united funds. Under this scheme united funds provide the "lost dollars." Agencies least aggressive in securing client fee and other earned and contributed income, or with the least efficient operation, tended to require and receive the largest united fund allocations.

Finally, management positions have generally been filled by promoting social workers from practice or supervisory positions. The effects of this staffing pattern have been to narrow the focus of agency operations to a single or at most a few problems or service techniques and to direct major management attention to perfecting service-provision techniques. While the latter is an essential and urgent management concern, it has overshadowed other essential concerns. Long-term planning, marketing, and financing were neglected. A strategy for private financing, to say nothing of a strategy for retaining or expanding the private agency market share, has been slighted if not ignored.

The Organization

Lutheran Social Services of Wisconsin and Upper Michigan (LSS) was organized in 1936. By mergers it acquired in 1938 a Milwaukee institutional chaplaincy program dating from 1918 and in 1936 two children's institutions dating from the 1880s. LSS participated in the history summarized above. Enormous efforts were made to professionalize services and insure their effectiveness.

Distinctively, however, the agency has from the beginning been oriented to marketing.

The first LSS employee was a promotion secretary charged with presenting need, selling agency services, and raising funds in the sponsoring congregations. Further, the agency committed itself early to involvement in community and government policy development. It participated from the start in so-called community-service planning efforts. This outward orientation contributed importantly to the development of agency management style. It has stood where the winds were blowing and by the fifties was seeking to apply scientific management to its operations. Without exception, the four executive directors who have headed the organization came to the position without extensive direct-service experience.

Along with comparable Lutheran agencies, particularly in the Midwest, LSS enjoyed steady growth. It now is a multifunction social agency providing counseling for individual and family problems, residential treatment of emotionally disturbed adolescents and related outpatient services for their families, foster care and adoption, institutional chaplaincy, clinical education for professionals, consultation, social change, public education services, and volunteer services.

LSS employs approximately 165 staff and has an operating budget of $2.5 million. In round numbers, government purchases of service in various forms and contracts provide 50 percent, some 25 united funds 10 percent, client fees 10 percent, church sources 25 percent, individual, foundation, corporation, and miscellaneous 5 percent of its operating income.

The managerial group comprises seven managers at three levels. Middle management comprises eight area administrators and an additional number of first-line supervisors, all of whom also carry some direct service responsibilities.

Services are delivered through nine offices, seventeen satellite offices manned on a full- or part-time basis, two major institutions, five small residences. Additional office locations and specialized treatment residences are in development.

Clientele numbers some 5,000 receiving basic therapeutic services. Additional thousands are helped by agency-provided or -related chaplaincy services. The agency also relates to a church constituency of one-half million and maintains broad contacts with government, community, and educational organizations and groups.

History of the MBO Installation

In the early 1960s, LSS began a long-range planning effort with the leadership and heavy involvement of the executive director. The effort produced a statement of agency mission and basic policies to guide its service program and staff development and financing. The agency is presently moving toward a full MBO program installation. The installation will capitalize on various other agency management components.

The reactivated long-range planning effort in the early 1970s produced the following restatement of agency mission, which was adopted by the board of directors:

> Lutheran Social Services of Wisconsin and Upper Michigan is a social agency through which Lutheran church members, congregations, and jurisdictions act in obedience and witness to the love of Jesus Christ.
>
> The agency selects and works in areas of human need in order to:
>
>> Enrich and salvage families and the lives of individual children and adults;
>>
>> Strengthen and promote the responsiveness of social institutions to changing conditions;
>>
>> Encourage and support the renewal of the church in its concern for individuals and society.
>
> The agency pursues these purposes as a servant and a leader and in cooperation with other service organizations. It functions through the efforts of qualified employed and volunteer personnel working under appropriate professional direction within limits that assure high standards of effectiveness.

Service definitions, completed by 1970, are a basic building block for a service agency MBO program. They provide a focus for professional staff effort und collection points for service statistics. At LSS these statistics include such data as client intake and service volumes, days of care for residential services, staff output of direct client contact hours. A typical service definition is that for family-life education, first in the systems manual form and then in the staff statistical recording guide:

> *Title: Family Life Education Services*
> Definition: Activities or programs which utilize the educational process to anticipate and prevent family stress and to enrich family and social relationships and the ability to deal with problems of family living; to strengthen the family unit.

Family Life Education: Providing and presenting programs to groups and/or organizations designed to strengthen the relationship of the family and its ability to deal with problems of family living.

Also, in the early 1970s a system of measuring staff output in direct contact hours and of stating unit costs of service was applied.

Concurrently the executive director, with wide board, management, and staff input, formulated corporate five-year goals and one- or two-year objectives. In the first several years, these statements were replete with "expand," "increase," "improve" terminology. The most recent statement which follows is far more specific in language and quantities. A reference document that accompanies the goals and objectives statement cites the statistical base-line data for quantities, and states assumptions and rationale that underlie the instruction of the goals and objectives. Figure 23, which appears at the end of this chapter, sets forth the agency's long-range goals for the years 1975 to 1979 as well as the 1975 objectives.

Corporate goals and objectives, which, as mentioned, are developed through ongoing input from and cross checking with the agency board, management, and staff, are the basis for organizational unit and individual staff member objective setting. Equipping agency managers, supervisors, and staff with added knowledge and skill in objective formulation and achievement is a major program the agency plans to implement.

LSS moved to adapt and apply MBO as a means of setting priorities, of directing activities and efforts toward defined ends, and of measuring accomplishments. Further, the ability to secure adequate funding was recognized as dependent on identifying, stating, and verifying accomplishments. Since a service organization accomplishes only that which its first-line service staff accomplishes with agency clientele, objectives and funding are essential. Objectives are essential to staff self-direction and -motivation; funding, to monetary rewards of staff achievement.

As noted above, the refinement and installation of MBO continue. To date, staff training has been provided to accomplish application of service statistical and cost/income reporting systems. Orientation sessions for top and middle managers have introduced MBO concepts. In one residential treatment unit an entire staff has participated in developing and applying EVAL-U-TREAT, a modified and elaborate MBO procedure. This procedure is being applied selectively to particular services in several other locations. Annual staff discussions have been held on the application of corporate goals and objectives. Unit and individual objectives have been prepared and accepted throughout the agency. Objectives for 1975 included installation of a formal management by results system through the first-line supervisors.

The process of writing the first set of goals and objectives took approximately four months in 1972. Initial application throughout the agency required an additional three to four months. Time intervals in succeeding years have been approximately the same. The major effort to restate the agency's mission required more than two years of work by a planning committee, with extensive discussions and feedback from board, management, and staff as the work proceeded.

As is evident in the statement of current goals and objectives, quoted earlier, a major shift to concrete, measurable quantity statements has been achieved. Policy statements incorporated in earlier drafts have been essentially eliminated. These have been included in part in a new statement of policies to guide agency development and will be included in future operating policy statements.

Description of MBO Installation

The current MBO installation is used to carry out four major functions:

1. Set the basic direction of agency service development, delivery, and funding.
2. Establish the basis for agency service and fiscal budgets.
3. Determine and direct the activity of agency personnel.
4. Evaluate the performance of agency personnel.

To some extent and in at least some limited forms the application has been made at all management levels including first-line supervision. For example, a supervisor in an institutional unit that has given little or no formal consideration to MBO is nonetheless aware of his responsibility for achieving service volume, intake, discharges, successful treatment, and the like. The board and practically all agency professional staff have participated in small group discussions that evaluated present and proposed corporate goals and objectives and suggested modifications and additions. Almost every professional staff member has in at least a primitive way set personal objectives in relation to corporate objectives.

The executive director, who is the agency's chief executive officer, takes personal responsibility for formulating corporate goals and objectives for the board's approval. (He also drafted the statement of long-term purpose or mission). He provides overall direction to their application. As pointed out repeatedly, the process of formulation includes a year-round, systematic review and input process in which board, management, and staff actively participate. A principal resource group to the executive director in this work is the long-range planning committee consisting of carefully chosen persons including two board, two staff, and two outside members.

The day-to-day execution of the MBO program is the responsibility of the associate executive director for program services and the associate executive director for management services. The latter, in particular, is charged with developing and operating the data feedback system.

Problems or Special Situations

The basic problem in applying MBO in a social service organization is identifying and stating measurable results or outputs of intangible services. The achievement to date (stating staff outputs in days of care or direct contact hours provided to clients) will no doubt remain a continuing part of the system, but it cannot be regarded as final. The true measure of agency output and effectiveness is consumer change and satisfaction. It is this matter that EVAL-U-TREAT particularly addresses. A further application and refinement of MBO for general use in the agency must include this feature.

A variety of specific problems have required and will require concerted attention and effort. A major problem is achieving staff competence in formulating objectives. This competence must be acquired while resistance to devoting time to planning and objective setting is handled and overcome.

The further elaboration and refinement of the agency data system is necessary to arrive at reliable data bases for objective setting and results measurement. However, the fact that we now have a clearly stated purpose or mission as well as goals and objectives provides an indispensable means for determining what should be known—what data should be collected. Now that we have a better idea of where we want to go, we are better able to mark the way with readable way posts.

Finding an appropriate blend of specificity and generality in goals and objectives statements requires continuing experimentation and evaluation. Along with this problem, the identification of appropriate quantities, referred to earlier, is yet to be achieved. Perhaps these and other problems can never be fully solved, but their impact can, at least, be lessened.

Hindsight

Much earlier it might have been helpful to restudy and revise the agency organization structure. Fewer management and supervisory layers and possibly fewer management and supervisory positions as well as clearer, well-defined delegations would have made the transition to MBO smoother and more effective.

Stronger direction from the executive director to insure a better-organized, more adequately staffed, highly disciplined, and tightly scheduled training program for agency managers would have sped up and upgraded the introduction of MBO. Again, however, it is important to recognize that the very introduction of objectives furnishes the basis for this insight.

Evaluation of Results to Date

Currently the agency has become oriented to the achievement of results. The sense of simply doing one thing after another has been superseded by at least some evident sense of direction and effort to accomplish something specific. The whole character of the agency is being reshaped by a theological orientation that arises from MBO.

Much of course remains to be done. A preliminary step may be some reshaping of the agency's structure. Another necessary step, also under way, is the computerization of the service and fiscal data system. The agency's size and activity volume preclude continued hand processing of data.

More specifically, further installation of MBO will require the selection of a consultant to work with agency managers and supervisors. Their additional training is a key to future progress. One expected result of such training will be refined corporate goals and objectives as well as unit and individual objectives.

A compensation that will more closely correlate achieved results and individual salaries is recognized as badly needed. Some preliminary investigation of this subject has been started.

Areas of Dissatisfaction

There are of course dissatisfactions. The long interval between the executive director's first introduction to MBO concepts in Peter Drucker's writings (first read in the late 1950s) and the present introductory installation of MBO is a long time indeed. The continuing series of upheavals and crises in funding and staffing the agency, to say nothing of determining program direction, have contributed ongoing frustrations. Nothing seems to ever get done on time! The length of time it seems to take to simply understand a thing like MBO, and figuring out how to get it going in an organization, is discouraging to say the least.

The ability to identify and define significant, measurable results comes too slowly. The primitive state of management knowledge in the service field contributes to this problem. It appears that much frustrating work lies ahead before we can be reasonably sure that key results are identified and indicators of achievement stated and quantified.

Major Successes

LSS has achieved a consciousness of purpose, character, and identity. This is particularly evident in the board and at the upper management levels. We at least now sense where the issues are and what the argument is about.

Managers particularly have become aware of how today's actions and decisions determine the agency's character tomorrow. Seldom, if ever, for example, is a new service proposal or a new contract considered without reference to agency purpose, objectives, and service definitions. Policy has come alive.

The organization is oriented to measurable results. In evaluating a staff member's performance, for example, the relative weight to be given to direct contact hour output may be argued, but at least it is considered. Administrators' responsibility to achieve client fee income as well as client service levels is clearly accepted.

Finally, MBO has enabled LSS to become more honest and forthright about its intentions. We now say directly that we want to grow—something many church leaders and people are reluctant to desire or state.

Managerial Time Requirements

The executive director has, on estimate, directed from one-fourth to one-third of his time to planning, goal and objective setting, and direction of implementation. This time allocation is seen as an essential requirement of effective agency operations now and for the future.

The board of directors invests about one-third of its time to considering goals and objectives or in evaluating their achievement.

Management, supervisory, and professional service-providing staff devote an estimated one-fourth of their time spent in supervision to direct MBO-related activity. This time goes into formulating objectives, determining how to accomplish them, and discussing achievement.

Costs

We have no reliable cost estimates. However, we believe that while initial time investments were great, the economies in knowing what we are doing more than offset the investment. Since 1970, productivity has increased. Unit costs have been held constant or in some instances have even declined despite inflation. The agency has been generally price- and quality-competitive in retaining old business and securing new contract business. It has generally enjoyed increased church-contributed income that exceeded increases to congregations and national causes.

Special Problems for a Nonprofit Enterprise

A major problem for nonprofit enterprises is orienting the board of directors, management, and staff to think in terms of outputs and results, as opposed to simply holding expenditures within the limits of income. The understanding of the nature of service activity—the comprehension of expectation—is so undeveloped that there is little to go on. Thus there is a requirement for first creating and then communicating the most basic concepts of service and its measurement.

The second problem is closely related to the first and has been referred to in several places above: finding or creating and defining tangible, quantitative measurements for intangible service products or outputs. Again, this is a major area for development.

The elaboration of the second problem leads to a third: finding, if possible, reliable measures of the ultimate results of services in individual human lives and in society. Here is a profound, perhaps insoluble problem. But, as increasingly large proportions of our human and natural resources are directed to providing services, this problem looms large, forbidding, but urgent.

Figure 23. Long-range goals and objectives, 1975–1979.

GOAL I   1975–1979: Agency Character

Continue to develop the overall character of the agency in a manner that expresses its relationship with the church, and continues to affirm its commitment to the integration of the Christian faith in agency operations through at least one annual general program of theological orientation and through ongoing application of Christian theology in agency services.

A. 1975 Objective: Theological Orientation

   Provide for the board, committees, and staff at least <u>one</u> significant orientation program on the Christian theological basis of the agency's purpose and program.

B. 1975 Objective: Theological Application

   State the basis in Christian theology and its manner and indicators of application in practice for at least <u>two</u> agency-defined services.

GOAL II   1975–1979: Agency Program and Funding

Increase the volume of agency services at a steady rate of <u>6–8</u> percent annually.

1975 Objectives: Agency Funding

1. Increase the aggregate income from church congregation and jurisdictional sources and the aggregate income from united funds for 1975 in relation to the inflation rate in that year to at least maintain the number of staff positions or the amount of service supported by these funds.
2. Increase the income from individual, corporate, and foundation sources by <u>15</u> percent over the average 1972–1974 actual.
3. Increase client fee income by at least <u>6</u> percent over 1974 actual.

4. Increase government funding of agency services funded by this source in 1974 by at least 10 percent.
5. Institute at least one third-party prepayment plan (insurance coverage for social services) for agency service.

1975 Objectives: Program Services

1. Counseling Services
   Increase volume by 10 percent over the 1974 direct contact hour service budget, adjusted for contracts added during the year.
2. Problem Pregnancy
   Provide service at level of client demand, but not above the 1974 direct contact hour service budget.
3. Foster Care and Group Homes for Children.
   (a) Increase foster care service by 10 percent as a resource to whole family service over 1974 actual direct contact hours.
   (b) Open 4 group homes in response to local needs.
4. Adoption
   (a) Place all normal infants for adoption within an average of 5 days of transfer of guardianship to the agency.
   (b) Place not less than 50 percent more handicapped, older, or foreign children in adoptive homes than were placed in 1974.
5. Residential Treatment
   (a) Achieve 88 percent occupancy levels of operating capacity.
   (b) Relocate one MLH cottage into two community treatment units.
   (c) Carry out at least one new experimental or program development project each at MLH and HHB.
6. Consultation to Professionals
   (a) Provide at 1974 actual direct contact hour level.
   (b) Provide not less than 60 percent of this service to ALC-LCA pastors and lay professionals.
7. Community Planning and Program Coordination
   Provide at the 1974 actual direct contact hour level, but direct activity essentially to achieving agency fiscal and service goals and objectives.
8. Professional and Technical Education
   (a) Provide at 1974 actual level.
   (b) Involve not less than 50 ALC-LCA pastors and lay persons in a planned, significant professional or technical educational experience.
9. Social Improvement Services
   (a) Increase volume by 70 percent over 1974 budgeted direct contact hour level.
   (b) Expend not less than 65 percent of staff direct contact hours for this service with ALC-LCA congregations.
   (c) Involve not less than 70 ALC-LCA congregations in planned active, ongoing social change efforts.
   (d) Expend not more than 25 percent of staff direct contact hours for this service in personal staff efforts toward social change.
   (e) Expend not more than 10 percent of staff direct contact hours for this service with various religious and community officials and groups to further their involvement in social change.
   (f) Expend not less than 60 percent of staff direct contact hours on the major social issue to which agency resources are committed on a long-term basis, and not more than 40 percent of such hours on concerns of an immediate nature.

10. Family Life Education

   (a) Provide family life education offered directly to clients by agency staff at the actual 1974 direct contact hour level.

   (b) Extend family life education by assisting not less than <u>100</u> ALC-LCA congregations—individually or in clusters—to develop and conduct annually repeated family care and enrichment programs.

11. Institutional Chaplaincy

   (a) Enable the establishment of not less than <u>3</u> new paid chaplaincy positions in institutions or organizations in Wisconsin and Upper Michigan.

   (b) Increase the number of institutions with ongoing volunteer ALC-LCA pastor or lay chaplaincy programs by <u>25</u> percent over the number functioning at the end of 1974.

12. Public Education

   (a) Provide education on agency services through printed materials in all Wisconsin and Upper Michigan ALC-LCA congregations.

   (b) Provide education on agency services through visual materials in:

   All ALC congregations.

   <u>20</u> percent of LCA congregations.

   (c) Provide education on agency services through personal presentations in not less than <u>20</u> percent of ALC and LCA congregations.

   (d) Provide education on agency services to not less than <u>40</u> significant community groups through personal presentations.

13. Volunteer Services

   Involve volunteers in providing not less than one-eighth of a day of time per week for each agency full-time paid position to work in agency client or management services (as distinct from ALC-LCA members in congregation-agency social action, chaplaincy, and family life services).

1975 Objective: Productivity

   Achieve overall direct contact hour service output of <u>65</u> percent of total service staff clock hours through an individualized application of this objective to agency professional staff positions.

1975 Objective: Service Growth

   Identify and select <u>one</u> new area of service with high growth and income potential for initiation in the following year.

GOAL III   1975–1979: Agency Effectiveness

Improve the overall effectiveness of the agency program by introducing evaluation indicators in at least <u>3</u> defined agency services and by establishing and achieving accompanying standards of effectiveness.

1975 Objectives

1. Expend an average of <u>2</u> percent of total agency paid staff clock hours of time in acquiring knowledge and skill in relation to the achievement of agency goals and objectives.

2. Install a management by results system applied to at least the first level of supervision, to be operational by the tenth month of the year.

GOAL IV   1975–1979: Agency Staffing

Maintain overall staffing with a turnover rate for full-time staff of not more than <u>15</u> percent overall and with an average tenure of not less than <u>4</u> years for staff leaving the agency.

1975 Objectives

1. Process at least <u>90</u> percent of all staff or board suggestions for changes in personnel policy through the Personnel Committee and as appropriate through the board within <u>one</u> year.
2. Refine agency quality and quantity performance expectations through the ongoing review and redefinition of individual staff objectives.

GOAL V   1975–1979: Agency Organization

Achieve at least <u>80</u> percent participation by agency organizational units in significant projects requiring intraagency collaboration of effort between such organizational units; achieve at least <u>3</u> significant annual instances of agency involvement in interorganization collaboration.

1975 Objectives

1. Identify, plan, and carry out intraagency collaboration involving <u>60</u> percent of agency organizational units.
2. Identify and carry out at least <u>3</u> interorganization collaborative efforts involving cooperation with other organizations and with Lutheran organizations involving possible future consolidation.

15

case study

MBO
in Church Organizations

Renewal by objectives (RBO) is a team approach designed to help us better plan, organize, and carry out His work so that we may be better stewards of our time, talent, and efforts in achieving the most desirable results for God, our church, and ourselves. As alternatives, we might also call the approach ministry by objectives or stewardship by objectives.

First, we decide what we want our church to accomplish or where we want our church to be in the future.

Next, we develop an order of priorities. Which are the more important things we should do? Which should be done first? Which will result in greater benefit to the church?

Then we express these priorities in the form of objectives— the results we must achieve to carry out our stewardship.

Author's comment: This chapter describes an MBO installation made in a large Protestant church organization in the Midwest in which I served as a consultant. It also illustrates the step-by-step method of arriving at meaningful objectives that can be used by any organization.

After our objectives have been established, we develop plans to achieve them. The objectives tell us *what* we want to achieve, the plans tell *how* we plan to achieve the objectives. Plans are the step-by-step explanation of the ways in which the objective will be accomplished.

Once the objectives and plans have been agreed to and we start carrying them out, we must review our progress from time to time to make sure that satisfactory progress is being made. This progress review helps us answer the questions: "Are we successfully carrying out our objectives and plans? Is it necessary to revise them?"

The value of the "team approach" lies in the proven fact that the more actively people become involved and participate in the work of the church, the more successful the church will become in carrying out its mission. The church "team" includes its pastor, its governing body, and its congregation. The congregation is especially vital to the success of RBO because, unlike the situation in many other types of organizations, the congregation is the body that must ultimately approve or pass on the totality of the results.

Why RBO?

Most people want to see their church progress and grow. They want to do good work. They want to contribute to the church's progress in the most meaningful and rewarding manner possible.

Yet we know that some churches are more effective than others. Why? While there are probably several answers to this question, two are particularly significant to RBO.

One involves how we use our time. The other centers around how we plan and organize our efforts. Both are interrelated.

Ernest Hemingway admonished us to "never mistake motion for action." Also, we've heard people say, "He's always busy, but he never seems to get anything done." Both quotations are pertinent.

The best way to squander our precious time and effort is to become busy trying to accomplish something without first determining what it is we want to accomplish. It's rather like a postman running around trying to deliver a letter that doesn't have a name and address on the envelope.

The people in one church may stay very busy carrying out a

great many activities and *hoping* that something good will happen. (This is not RBO.)

The people in a second church determine what they want to happen and then align all their efforts to *make* it happen. (This is RBO.)

Thus an overwhelming reason for practicing renewal by objectives is to help us accomplish the most meaningful and rewarding results for our church by first determining the most important things we want to do, by directing all the individual efforts of our team toward the things we want to accomplish, and by avoiding spending our time and energy on efforts that are not needed. Emphasis is on the results we want to achieve, not on the unorganized efforts expended.

RBO helps replace "motion sickness" with a sense of purpose and direction. Under RBO we don't get on board a ship and run around in circles hoping it will take us someplace. Instead, we first determine where we want to go and then steer a course to reach that point.

"Ownership"—the Key to Success

RBO requires active involvement and participation by all members of a church. The pastor, the governing body, and the congregation—all must be actively involved and participate together to further the church's work.

Study after study has demonstrated that a person will not be really committed to helping achieve a result unless he has had a voice in determining what the result will be. Conversely, people will be more motivated to work for the success of a project if they have had a part in developing it.

Thus high commitment and high motivation usually go hand in hand with the degree to which a person believes that it is his or her project—that he or she "owns" it. "Ownership," therefore, is a big part of the foundation of successful RBO.

The late Douglas McGregor, one of the most respected behavioral scientists, emphasized the need for blending the efforts and the interest of the individual (the church member) with those of the organization (the church) when he wrote:

> Man will exercise self-direction and self-control to reach objectives to which he is committed. The most significant rewards, the satisfaction of ego and self-actualization needs, can be direct products of ef-

fort directed toward organizational objectives. The average human being learns, under proper conditions, not only to accept but to seek responsibility. The capacity to exercise a relatively high degree of imagination, ingenuity, and creativity in the solution of organizational problems is widely, not narrowly, distributed in the population. Under the conditions of modern industrial life, the intellectual potentialities of the average human being are only partially utilized.[1]

Dr. McGregor's findings highlight the value of participation to any organized group endeavor. A high degree of participation usually leads to an increased feeling of ownership. Thus all members of the church must feel they have a major voice in determining the future of their church, that they really "own" the church.

The RBO System

RBO is referred to as a system because it has several integrated components. Each must be present and must fulfill its role if the sum total is to work. The components of the RBO system are:

Establishing objectives.
Developing step-by-step plans to achieve the objectives.
Carrying out the plans.
Reviewing progress as the plans progress.
Revising objectives and plans to keep them realistic.

Much like any other system, if any of these five components is missing or if it is not carrying out its proper role, the system will suffer and the desired results will not be achieved.

The Sequence in Setting Objectives

Figure 24 illustrates the step-by-step process for establishing objectives for a local church. Also, it indicates who in the church is primarily responsible for carrying out each of the three major phases in the sequence.

Here again, as in the section on ownership, it is emphasized

[1] *The Human Side of Enterprise* (New York: McGraw-Hill, 1960).

Figure 24. The objective-setting process in an autonomous local church.

PHASE I

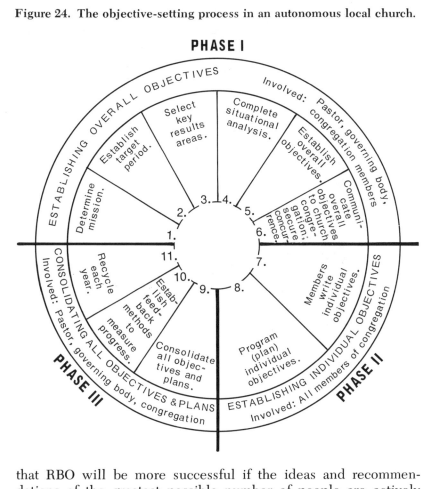

that RBO will be more successful if the ideas and recommendations of the greatest possible number of people are actively sought and considered in each step of the whole process.

A high premium should be placed on getting maximum involvement by *all* members of the congregation.

Phase I Establishing Overall Objectives

The first step in the objective-setting process is to establish overall objectives for the total church for a particular period of time. Usually these are established by a working committee comprising the pastor and the governing body. The more in tune these people are with the ideas and views of the congregation, the more successful the whole approach will usually be—especially concerning objectives that will require the later support and work by members of the congregation. This requires extensive communication and coordination with the congregation while formulating the church objectives.

The following step-by-step procedure is used to arrive at the overall objectives of the church:

Step 1: Determine the church's mission.

Step 2: Establish the target period.

Step 3: Select the "key results areas" in which it is necessary to ultimately establish objectives for insuring the future growth and progress of the church. (These are the major "thrust" or "initiative" areas.)

Step 4: Complete a situational analysis to analyze our capability to achieve results in each of the key subject areas.

Step 5: Establish the objectives.

Step 6: Secure concurrence by the congregation of the objectives.

Once the overall objectives for the total church have been established and agreed to, they provide (1) a commitment for the total church (they state what all of the members working together must accomplish) and (2) overall guidance and direction for all members of the church as they establish their individual objectives to make the overall church objectives come true.

It is important to remember that the overall objectives for the church as a whole are not the responsibility of any one individual but, rather, the collective responsibility of all. To get action on these objectives they must be translated into individual objectives that enumerate who is responsible for what, and when. This is discussed in Step 7.

Step 1: Mission

The objective-setting process begins with the definition of the total purpose of the church. A mission statement should not be so broad that it provides little, if any, guidance, as in this example: "Our mission is to carry out God's work." This statement is so broad that it provides almost no guidance as to the areas on which the church should concentrate.

Similarly, the mission statement should not be so restrictive that it overly confines the purpose of the church. An example of an overly restrictive statement might read: "Promote a moral and spiritual atmosphere conducive to the well-being of our youth."

A balanced statement that provides a happy medium will probably include answers to these questions:

1. What part of God's work do we want our church to accomplish?
2. What is our reason for being?
3. What is our purpose?
4. What geographical area should we serve?
5. What people should the church serve?
6. What services should the church provide?

Step 2: Establish the Target Period

The target period is the length of time for which it is decided to plan and set objectives. Normally we are concerned with two target periods: long-range, which commonly means three years or more, and short-range, one year or less. Normally, long-range objectives are set first. This helps insure the growth of the church over the long pull and provides guidance as to what objectives should be set for the short-range. The short-range objectives that are set within the context and guidance of the long-range objectives are the steps by which the long-range ones will be achieved; for example: A long-range objective might involve the building of a new church, which may take three years.

Annual objectives are then set to make certain the three-year objective is achieved. Examples:

First year: Secure funds and design the church.

Second year: Complete one-half of church construction.

Third year: Complete the remaining construction.

Step 3: Select Key Results Areas

These are the major areas in which the church must achieve results during the target period if it is to survive and/or progress. They may also be referred to as the keys to success—the areas in which high performance is necessary for success. Key results areas for a typical church might include:

1. Level of membership.
2. Level and sources of funds.
3. Neighborhood acceptance.

4. Youth participation.
5. Membership participation.
6. Worship facilities.
7. Quality of leadership.
8. Quality of services.

Step 4: Complete a Situational Analysis

In this step we analyze our capability to achieve results in each of the key results areas, which we selected in Step 3. One way to do this is to take each key result area, one at a time, and discuss it in light of strengths, weaknesses, opportunities, and threats.

For example, in the first key result area (level of membership) strengths might be excellent facilities, central location, and the like. Weaknesses might be a highly mobile congregation and a high percentage of working families in the neighborhood. Two excellent opportunities could be a growing neighborhood combined with limited social and leisure-time activities outside of church. Major threats might be the possible closing of defense-related companies and a general lessening of faith and belief in religion.

A thoroughly completed situational analysis, on each of the key results areas, should provide us with excellent guidance as to what kinds of objectives we should write in Step 5. For example, the strengths and weaknesses should give us a picture of our current situation; that is, what we have to work with. They should help us answer the questions: (1) Should we have objectives that will help us capitalize on our strengths? (2) Do we need objectives to minimize our weaknesses?

The opportunities and threats are future-oriented. Questions we should ask include: (1) Should we have objectives to help us take advantage of our opportunities? (2) Do we need objectives to help us minimize the impact of the threats?

Step 5: Establishing Objectives

Having determined the major directions that we want our church to take and having arrived at a prioritized list of the key results areas in which we want to achieve better results, we are now ready to begin writing objectives. *Example:* "We have determined that one of the key results areas which we want to concentrate on during 1975 is a higher degree of participation by the congregation in church activities."

The next step is to write an objective covering this key subject area.

What is an objective? For our purposes, we may define an objective as a specific statement of an end result to be achieved during a stated period of time.

An objective should always include the *what* (the end result) and the *when* (a target period or target date). *Example:* "Our key result area is a higher degree of participation by the congregation in church activities."

The resulting objective might read: "By December 31, 1975, increase Sunday school attendance by a monthly average of 10 percent above the monthly average for 1974."

The date of December 31, 1975, tells by *when* the objective will be achieved. The 10 percent increase tells the *what*.

Two main categories of objectives. Although there are several different categories of objectives we might consider, the two we are interested in here we may refer to as unit objectives and individual objectives.

Unit objectives apply to the church as a whole (or to a unit of it). They are not the objectives of any one individual but are broader objectives of the organization. They set the theme and direction and provide guidance for writing individual objectives. *Example:* "Increase total church membership by one hundred people by July 1, 1975."

Individual objectives, as the name implies, are objectives that apply to an individual—those that he will personally carry out. *Example:* "Personally secure ten new church members by July 1, 1975."

Individual objectives usually are a smaller piece of unit objectives. When the individual objectives of all members of a unit are added together, they should result in achieving the broader unit objective. *Example:* "The unit objective is to secure one hundred new members; the individual objective is for ten members of the congregation to secure ten new members each."

Making objectives effective. Effective objectives should meet several criteria. They should be specific and measurable, realistic and attainable, supportive, clearly understood, have priorities assigned, and be in writing.

1. *Specific and measurable.* An objective is specific and measurable when it states exactly what is to be achieved and when

progress can be gauged in the most accurate terms. *Example* (poor): "Increase church membership." This is merely a statement of intent; it is not specific and measurable.

The intent could be achieved by securing only one new member or by one hundred members. What do we mean? Better: "By July 1, 1975, achieve total minimum church membership of 200 (from present level of 163) and maintain at the 200 level for the remainder of 1975."

When an objective is not specific, it cannot be measured for accomplishment, we cannot formulate plans to achieve it, and we won't know what resources we will need to carry it out.

2. *Realistic and attainable.* Objectives should require us to expend more than just normal effort; they should require us to "stretch" to reach them. However, objectives should always be realistic and attainable.

The key word is "realism." Objectives that are based on hopes, desires, and wishes are seldom realistic.

3. *Supportive.* Once unit objectives have been set for the church as a whole, the objectives of all members should be established in a manner that helps carry out the church's objectives.

4. *Clearly understood.* Before starting to carry out an objective, all persons involved must clearly understand what the objective requires and what their respective roles are. Otherwise, confusion, misunderstanding, and misdirected effort will frequently result.

5. *Ranked by priority.* Like many other organizations, a church has a limit on the time and funds it can expend. Therefore, we want to make certain we are devoting our resources to the most important things and that the most important are done first. Objectives should cover these more important subjects in our work.

6. *Written form.* Objectives should always be written, to promote better understanding and to avoid confusion.

Step 6: Enunciate and Secure Concurrence with Overall Church Objectives

Once the pastor and the governing body have agreed to the broad, overall objectives of the church as a whole (for a particular target period), these objectives are announced, discussed, and clarified with the congregation. The greatest possible effort should be exerted to secure overwhelming concurrence by the congregation. The success of any of these overall objectives will depend heavily upon congregational enthusiasm and support.

The objectives provide members of the congregation with the guidance they will need to write their individual objectives, which will support and help carry out the overall objectives.

Phase II   Establishing Individual Objectives

Step 7: Writing Individual Objectives

In this step, the members of the congregation write objectives for themselves, using the overall objectives written in Step 6 as guidance.

The individual objectives should support the overall objectives and should be written in the light of the criteria discussed in an earlier section, "Making Objectives Effective."

Step 8: Programming Objectives

In this phase of RBO we develop the step-by-step plans that we will follow to achieve the objectives we have written. The objective tells *what* we are going to accomplish.

Now we are concerned with the *how*—how are we going to make the objectives come true? Plans are developed in the following order:

1. *State the objective.* "Increase church membership to 200 persons by December 31, 1975."

2. *Select all practical alternatives.* There are many ways in which we might accomplish our objective. We list as many as possible of the more practical ones. They might include:

Home visits by members.
Newspaper advertising.
Visits by pastor.
Invitations to social events.
Recommendations/invitations by present members.
Mailing of newsletter describing church events.
Others.

3. *Evaluate the alternatives.* This step consists in examining each alternative. The purpose is to boil down the list to those we want

to adopt and those we want to program out. Each alternative should be examined in light of questions such as:

Is it practical—will it help us reach the objective?
What will it cost?
Have we the resources (people, time, money) to carry it out?
Is there a better alternative(s) that we might follow?
Others.

4. *Select the better alternatives.* Next, let's assume we have decided that the alternatives we will follow are home visits by members and recommendations by members. Each of these would then be programmed step by step.

5. *Program out the alternatives.* The first alternative might be programmed out as shown in Figure 25.

Phase III   Consolidating All Objectives and Plans

Step 9: *Consolidating Objectives and Plans*

The objective-setting process began with the setting, by the governing body and the pastor, of the broad, overall objectives of the church (hopefully, with the maximum possible recommendations and guidance from the congregation as to what these objectives should be).

Next these broad, overall objectives were enunciated to the congregation so that its members could participate in the total RBO system.

Using these objectives as guidance, members of the congregation established their own individual objectives to support and help carry out the overall church objectives.

Step 9 involves the combining and consolidating of all individual objectives into one "package." The key question that must be answered at this stage is: Will all the individual objectives and plans add up at least to the overall objectives of the church?

Expressed differently, if all the individual objectives and plans are carried out as written, will they result in the achievement of the broad, overall objectives of the church? If the answer is "yes," our job is fairly well completed. However, if the answer is "no," we have two alternative chores to complete:

1. We must establish additional plans and objectives to make

Figure 25. Plans to achieve objectives.

PERSON RESPONSIBLE: Chairman, Membership Committee

OBJECTIVE #1: Increase church membership to 200 by December 31, 1975

Major Action Steps	January – December											
	J	F	M	A	M	J	J	A	S	O	N	D
1. Visits by present members to homes of prospective members.	X											
1a. Appoint membership.		X										
1b. Determine strategy and approach.		X										
1c. Assign "quotas" to committee members.		X										
1d. Schedule the home visits.			X									
1e. Complete all home visits.				X								
1f. Committee meeting to review interim progress.					X							
1g. Hold orientation meeting at church for new prospects.						X						
1h. Induct new members.								X				
1i. Evaluate final results of membership drive.							X					

up for the void. This alternative should always be exhausted before lowering the overall church objectives.

2. We must change the broad, overall objectives of the church. Regardless of which alternative is pursued, we must conclude with objectives and plans that are *realistic* and *attainable*.

Step 10: Establishing Feedback to Measure Progress

This step is to decide when (how often) and how (with what methods) we will measure our progress as our target year begins and we start to carry out our objectives and plans.

Generally, we want to measure our progress often enough so that we will know at the earliest possible time if progress is not proceeding as planned. This permits us to take corrective action while there is still time left to take the action. If we waited until the end of the target period, there would be no time to do anything.

Therefore, interim or periodic checks during the target period are essential.

Step 11: Recycling Each Year

The last step in the process is completed each year for as long as the church is practicing renewal by objectives. We start all over with Step 1 and complete all the steps for the next target period.

16

case study

Department
of Veterans Affairs,
Canadian Government

Historically, bureaucracy is a decidedly useful social invention that emerged during the industrial revolution as a response to needs of industrial organizations for order and precision and the demands of workers for impartial treatment. It evolved as a mechanistic approach to organization and placed heavy reliance on a concept of power vested in position.

Thus in a typical bureaucracy there is a pyramidal hierarchy of authority levels in which decisions and orders are passed downward while only requested information flows upward. Upper levels control operations through a system of well-defined procedures and rules for dealing with all contingencies relating to work

Author's comment: Approximately three years ago, the executive branch of the Canadian federal government directed that all federal departments be managed by objectives. Several departments have made substantial progress in their MBO efforts. This chapter provides an overview of the DVA system and was contributed by The Honorable J. S. Hodgson, Deputy Minister, Department of Veterans Affairs.

activities. Ingenuity and innovation at lower levels tend to be viewed as threats to the order, stability, and authority structure that are fundamental to the organization. Promotion and selection are based more on technical competence than on managerial competence. Interpersonal relations are rather formal, with considerable regard for authority and status.

Bureaucracy served society well up to the midpoint of the twentieth century. Its strength lay in its great capacity to efficiently manage the routine and the predictable in human affairs. The bureaucratic model, which was characteristic of all institutional organizations, took particularly strong roots in government—and DVA was no exception.

The Era of Change

For many years, the bureaucratic model functioned effectively in DVA. Because the environment was relatively stable, departmental functions could be structured in terms of well-defined, continuing activities aimed at providing returning veterans with numerous rehabilitative services to help in their reestablishment as citizens of the community.

During the past decade, however, there have been revolutionary changes in the environment in which DVA was expected to provide such services. As federal and provincial governments began to play an increasing role in the health and welfare of all citizens, the veteran's dependence on DVA and the department's corresponding responsibilities toward him inevitably began to alter. Concurrently, there were sweeping changes in government organizational structures, management patterns, and operating methods. Most of these changes flowed from the Glassco Report of 1962 (a task force report presenting recommendations for improving government operations): decentralization, introduction of a program-planning-budgeting system (PPBS), collective bargaining, significant transfers of responsibility between the Treasury Board and the Public Service Commission, amendments to the Financial Administration Act, and abolition of the office of the Comptroller of the Treasury. Moreover, certain sociological trends during this period began to indicate an increasing dissatisfaction with traditional ways, and a desire for change. There was a growing insistence, spearheaded by the younger generation, that individuals have an inherent right to share in decisions that affect their lives. Organizations, too, experienced a growing sense of managerial self-awareness, as was clearly reflected in the spontaneity and spirit of our management by motivation seminars of 1969 and 1970, and by the rising expectations for improvement thus created.

These diverse influences called for an appropriate organizational response from the department. But managers found that their bureaucracy, with its nicely defined chain of command, its rules and its rigidities, could not effectively react to the rapid change the environment now demanded. Senior management became increasingly concerned with this deficiency and began exploring the possibility of some more dynamic and responsive approach to management. Oddly enough, the virtues of bureaucracy in an environment of stability and calm were the very characteristics that rendered it inappropriate and ineffective in a turbulent world of change.

This same phenomenon was recognizable elsewhere in government, as well as in private industry. To stimulate appropriate reforms, the Cabinet late in 1970 identified management improvement in the Public Service as priority problem No. 2.

Meeting the Challenge

Faced with growing demands arising from accelerating environmental change, and recognizing that the ills of bureaucracy were becoming more debilitating, managers began to perceive an answer in the results of rapidly expanding research in the behavioral, social, and management sciences. These findings pointed up a need to achieve fundamental changes in the basic philosophy that conditions managerial behavior, reflected particularly in three areas:

1. A new concept of *people* as individuals with complex and shifting needs, replacing the simplistic, push-button idea of man as a machine;
2. A new concept of *power* based on collaboration and reason, replacing the model of power based on coercion and fear;
3. A new concept of *organization* based on humanistic ideals, replacing the depersonalized, mechanistic value system of bureaucracy.

Over the past decade, large business firms in North America and Europe began developing new approaches to organization and management, trying to apply these emerging concepts through a blend of management and behavioral sciences that would supersede the bureaucratic model. The new models thus developed had several common characteristics:

1. An emphasis on managerial autonomy through decentralization of decision-making responsibility and authority.
2. A participative, teamwork management style.
3. A focus on results rather than activities.
4. A belief that the future is highly manageable.
5. A motivation flowing from individual identification with organization goals.
6. A conscious effort to develop creativity and innovation throughout the organization.
7. An atmosphere of open, frank, and trustful interpersonal relations.
8. An emphasis on the systems approach to the accomplishment of objectives.
9. A client orientation.

These early approaches were eminently successful, and the new way of managing spread rapidly. It went by various names—management by results, management by motivation, management by objectives, and various combinations of these titles.

In January 1971, the Cabinet gave impetus to this kind of management reform in the Public Service by endorsing management by objectives as a measure for achieving more effective and efficient management. The Treasury Board subsequently developed a strategy for reinforcing and coordinating the application of this new approach to management in six "pilot" departments. DVA, with change already under way as a consequence of the 1969–1970 MBM seminars, was one of these six.

In the summer of 1971, the department carried out a feasibility study. The report of this study provided the basis for subsequent management committee decisions as to the nature and extent of the changes to be introduced in DVA.

A first requirement was to determine and define with reasonable precision a concept of management by objectives appropriate to DVA.

The DVA Concept of MBO

In DVA, *management* is considered to be the key word in the MBO title; *management by objectives* is merely an indication of *how* to do it. The following definitions are given to clarify this fundamental management concept:

1. *Management* is viewed as a process whereby disorganized resources of men, machines, material, money, time, and space are integrated into a total system for accomplishing objectives.

2. *The job of the manager* is to create within the enterprise an environment that will facilitate the accomplishment of its objectives.

This concept of the management function is the foundation on which the departmental approach to managing by objectives has been developed. We believe that, if we are to have better management, we must first achieve a major transformation in our whole organizational culture; that is, changes in our organization structure and in climate, changes in our systems and processes of management, and changes in our beliefs, values, attitudes, and behavior.

So in DVA, management by objectives is much more than a goal-setting and review procedure tacked onto existing traditional processes of management. Instead, we see MBO as a way to realize a totally new kind of organizational life, one that is characterized by:

A climate of mutual trust, respect for the dignity and worth of others, frankness, candor, and collaboration;

An environment wherein each manager knows what is expected of him, wherein delegation, freedom to act, and authority to make decisions (and mistakes) are the norm, and wherein the manager is prepared to be accountable for results;

A spirit of vigor, venture, creativity, and innovation; and,

A systems approach in which the management process is viewed as a total system, in which the smaller subsystems are integrated with the whole, in which the fuctions of management (planning, organizing, directing, and controlling) are systematized, and in which the systems technology of modern management science is employed to maximum advantage.

Application of the Concept

Successful application of this DVA concept of MBO involves the creation of an organizational environment that develops entrepreneurs instead of agents, professional rather than amateur managers, a focus on the future not the past, an emphasis on results rather than activities, innovation and creativity instead of subservience to meticulous rules, reliance on self-direction and self-control in preference to the centralized control of a superior authority, and an overriding concern for the ultimate output in the form of client services. We see the building of such an environment as a process of organizational metamorphosis in which we will need to work together to bring about within ourselves and within our organization some far-reaching changes. These changes would have to do with our existing philosophies, attitudes, behavior, and management styles, and in interpersonal relationships throughout the organization; there will inevitably be significant changes as well in organization, in roles, and in technical systems.

To accomplish this, the department has embarked on a large-scale, long-term change program that will eventually touch every member and every facet of the department. Recognizing a need to provide guidance and coordination in the process of implementing this MBO change program, the management committee has adopted the following basic principles:

1. It is the responsibility of the manager to implement MBO within his area of accountability.

2. The department is not using any of the ready-made implementation systems offered for sale by several consulting firms. Primary reliance is placed on the development of in-house MBO advisers to act as "catalysts," and to provide staff assistance to managers. Such services may be reinforced by short-term contracts with professional consultants to meet special requirements.

3. Implementation should proceed from the top down through the successive levels of management, since each step in the implementation process has to be completed at one level before it can be effectively initiated at the next level.

4. MBO implementation can best be managed by objectives, with implementation goals set at each level of management and periodic reviews of progress toward their achievement.

5. Other management systems such as PPBS, employee evaluation, manager development, and the management information system are to be carefully phased into, and fully integrated with, the MBO system.

6. Because of the nature and magnitude of the changes involved, the pace of implementation should be one of deliberate

care. It is expected that the implementation process will require three to five years.

MBO is the most important initiative ever undertaken by the department in the field of improving managerial and organizational performance. Department managers individually and collectively have, in MBO, both the means and the opportunity for achieving organizational excellence.

17

MBO in
Other Organizations

Many other nonprofit organizations have MBO systems similar to those discussed in the previous case histories. A capsule view of a few of these is contained in the following paragraphs. The reader will undoubtedly by impressed with the wide range of endeavors represented by these organizations.

Schools

By virtue of their sheer weight of numbers and the importance of their end product—education—schools represent an area of prime concern with respect to first determining what their objectives should be and then coordinating all efforts to achieve those ends. Undoubtedly, this concern and the increasing burden on the taxpayer have caused the rather sudden surge of interest in applying MBO to schools. Probably no other category of nonprofit organization is receiving more MBO attention than are schools.[1]

[1] For a general discussion of applying MBO to schools, see H. Merrell Arnold,

Dr. Donald W. Shebuski, superintendent of schools of Holt, Michigan, is one of those most active in applying MBO to schools. He summarizes his experience as follows:

> School administrators have long endorsed the concept of a "management team." Recently, however, a managerial strategy, known as management by objectives, has assisted scientific-management-minded administrators to operationalize this team approach in education. Management by objectives is a method of participation and involvement of supervision and subordinates whereby decisions are reached and results explicated. Management at every level in schools has a continuing responsibility to improve the organization of the work under its supervision. It is accountable for the successful outcome of the team effort at any given level of responsibility.

> The key word in the MBO approach is "improve." A primary responsibility of a school administrator is to improve the work of the people he supervises, to improve the product (students), and to improve the team effort that makes the organization successful. Through successful accomplishment of the above, he also improves himself.

> Accomplishment of an accountability concept for schools means that we must explicate clearly defined goals, and have developed a management plan whereby goals can be reached in measurable ways.

> MBO is not a panacea for all of education's many problems, nor is it an attempt to turn schools into a mechanized factory-like process. It is a procedure in which scarce resources (people and dollars) can be allocated to accomplish established goals, and then account for the degree to which goals and objectives have been reached.

> Educational administrators have a great challenge before them as they face the durable concerns for accountability in education. At this point, educators are compelled to translate the educational process which, up until now has been considered an "art," into a viable, scientific procedure. Management by objectives processes are proving to be a successful approach in this endeavor.[2]

Government Laboratory

The U.S. Forest Products Laboratory, situated in Madison, Wisconsin, has recently completed a review of its first year of ap-

"Management by Objectives and the School System," *The School Administrator*, April 1972, pp. 15–16.

[2] Dale D. McConkey, "Applying Management by Objectives to Nonprofit Organizations," *SAM Advanced Management Journal*, January 1973.

plying management by objectives to its research management.[3] The results are gratifying, but there are many opportunities for continued expansion and improvement.

Although project management in research requires goals, and has been using them for many years, it was decided that management by objectives had some additional benefits that would be useful for all Forest Products research managers. The system was launched by first indoctrinating the top management group. Following this meeting, sessions were conducted for all project leaders and key scientists.

The mission of the laboratory, which was reviewed at the beginning of each session, was: "To conduct research leading to greater social and economic benefits for the people of the United States, and of the world, through the better utilization of their timber resources." The broad areas of concern of the laboratory were also reexamined during the sessions. Then each individual prepared objectives within the scope of his or her responsibilities consistent with the mission and within the following areas of concern:

1. The properties and behavior of wood and wood constituents.
2. Timber supply and utilization.
3. Efficiency in processing and use.
4. Better housing for the seventies.
5. The environment.
6. The rural economy.
7. Protection of wood in use.
8. Consumer interests.

Areas of improved management that the top management team has identified as a result of applying management by objectives include:

Clearer understanding of what is expected of research teams, project leaders, and individuals.

Specific connection between budget allocations and results accomplished on projects.

Increased involvement of entire staff in developing specific objectives to accomplish laboratory mission.

[3] This summary of the application of MBO in the U.S. Forest Products Laboratory was prepared by Professor Fred C. Schwarz, University of Wisconsin, Madison, who served as a consultant during the installation. It is used here with his permission as well as that of the management of the U.S. Forest Products Laboratory.

The management team is now managing by objectives.

The management team now has a common language, and has demonstrated its ability to attack a problem and approach it with a more positive attitude than before.

Canadian Post Office

Management by objectives was applied to the Canadian Post Office in January of 1970 beginning with a "pilot" project in the Ontario Region, one of the four large regions into which the postal system is divided. Subsequently, it was decided to extend MBO to all four regions and the headquarters of the system.

Several factors lay behind the decision to adopt MBO. The Canadian Post Office employed up to 50,000 people annually and was known as "the sleeping giant." Costs and deficits had mounted. Mail service, vital to both commerce and citizens, had been deteriorating. Increasing difficulty was being encountered in attracting competent personnel for key managerial positions.

A package of eight interrelated management programs was designed for the total planned change. The basis of these programs was the application of MBO, especially true delegation from the regional manager to the district manager to the area manager (the lowest level of management).

The experience gained in the pilot project leading up to the decision to adopt MBO for the total postal system showed that true delegation of accountabilities had taken place; that management in the Ontario Region was becoming stronger and more professional than the management at headquarters; and that the potential for systemwide application was so encouraging that the decision was made to waive the two-year trial period originally planned for the pilot project and to accelerate the systemwide adoption.

Management of the Canadian Post Office doesn't kid itself into believing that MBO is a panacea. A turnaround the size of this giant will take time. There is no quick, magic cure. However, management feels that now the organization has an approach that is sufficiently flexible to meet the dynamics of work even in the Post Office.[4]

___

[4] This summary of experience is adopted largely from "Business Planning in the Canadian Post Office," by P. J. Chartrand, *Canadian Personnel and Industrial Relations Journal*, October 1971, pp. 17–22. Used here with permission.

Hospitals

Plagued as they are with labor costs frequently averaging 70 to 80 percent of total operating cost, hospitals represent a fertile field for any management approach that promotes increased effectiveness. It seems only natural that hospitals have turned to MBO as a way of alleviating their plight.

Prior to assuming his present position as administrator of a large nonprofit hospital in Ottawa, Garry D. Cardiff played a significant role in applying MBO to another nonprofit hospital. In the following paragraphs, he summarizes the experience with MBO after three years:

1. Regardless of the effort put forth, enthusiasm and utilization of MBO are cyclic.
2. Only about 60 percent of those that started the program are still successfully using the approach. However, in light of factors such as background, personal limitations, and other organizational circumstances, this percentage seems acceptable to us.
3. The greatest enemy of an MBO program in a nonprofit organization is apathy. With the recent advent of "global budgeting," perhaps realistic incentive programs will be devised in a way that successful MBO performances can be rewarded in more tangible terms.
4. Many projects that "should be done" are done because of MBO. Procrastination generally is the result of lack of commitment.
5. The contribution to communications both horizontally and vertically has been immeasurable.
6. Contribution of MBO to our budgeting process has been equally rewarding.
7. Since MBO is an essential ingredient of writing and executing a long-range plan, the program will no doubt continue to prove invaluable, as we are currently in the primary stages of formulating such a plan.
8. On balance, the benefits we have gained far outweigh expenditures of time and money. Management by objectives is an interesting theory and a worthwhile practice.[5]

[5] Cardiff's experiences are described in his article "Management by Objectives—It Will Work in a Hospital Setting," *Hospital Administration in Canada,* November 1970, pp. 23–26.

Volunteer Organizations

Volunteer organizations are considered among the more difficult when applying MBO. However, the fact that an MBO application is possible is illustrated by the highlights of the experience of a large volunteer organization that, at this stage of development of its program, chooses to remain anonymous.

It operates nationally from a central headquarters, through regions, to local areas headed by a local manager, who represents the lowest level of management. Managers of all these levels are paid professionals. Managers of the local areas are the real guts of the organization, as they are accountable for fund raising, motivation of volunteers to carry out the bulk of the organization's work in the area, and effective direction of the local programs.

Strict standards of accountability have been established for the area managers. Their primary accountabilities are:

Program quantity
Program quality
Financial stability
Public relations
Internal relations

Each of these accountabilities is assigned a weight, or value, that reflects its importance to the manager's overall effectiveness. Commendably, quality is weighted in proportion to quantity.

Next, each accountability is defined in terms of standards of performance required. For example, the objective "program quantity" is spelled out in terms of the population size of the area, the percentage of the population represented by the age group that the organization seeks to bring into its program, the number of eligibles who actually participate in the program, and the percentage of total potential that this number represents. Program "quality" is defined and measured by factors such as the number of participants who stay in the program and how that compares with established medians.

The application now has endured several years of experience, and those to whom the organization is accountable are pleased with the results. The program emphasizes participation of all managers in setting their goals, strict accountability, measurement of performance and feedback to the managers, and maximization of the benefits provided for all funds raised.

Canadian Boy Scouts

Five years ago, the Boy Scouts of Canada was an organization in decline, holding onto a dwindling membership, recruiting few newcomers, and fast on its way to being a mere nostalgic memory of a charming small-town Canadian past.

Today the organization is vigorous, expanding, buoyant, and viable; it is launching into a number of innovative new programs that capture the interest of today's new urban generation.

How did this all happen? Stated very simply, through MBO. Concerned about the future of Boy Scouts, the top management group sought resort to MBO to reexamine traditional objectives and goals. They scrutinized the place of youth in today's society, designated key result areas that needed attention, set up a schedule of priorities, developed strategic and operational plans, innovated new programs, and put them into effect. The result: a dramatic case of institutional revitalization and recovery.

Learning the MBO approach was not easy, they report. The first year was particularly rough. But finally an MBO planning approach appropriate to Boy Scouts was worked out and successfully implemented. As with most new MBO attempts, perseverance was essential to success. But now it's all working and working well. The future looks great again, and the Scouts are truly "prepared" for next year, the next five years, and longer.[6]

Municipal Organizations

Often, a nonprofit organization has functions and operations that are identical with those existing in a profit-oriented one. The more common of these functions include purchasing, personnel, finance, administration, operations, and public relations. Organizations like municipal governments often have suborganizations that are almost duplicates of profit-making organizations—for example, the Port Authority of cities like Boston and New York. Madison, Wisconsin, has nine "enterprise funds," which include water utility, sewer utility, airport authority, bus utility, parking utility, golf courses, ice arena, concessions, and cemeteries. These funds are run on a consumer-reimbursement basis whereby costs are paid

[6] "Insights and Innovations for the Management of Change," *Management Concepts Limited*, September/October 1973, Scarborough, Ontario, Canada.

by the users. Each of these constitutes a minibusiness within the municipal government.

Certainly, these types of organizations readily lend themselves to MBO applications, and implementation is well under way in several instances.

Other Applications

The handful of examples described in the preceding paragraphs should not mislead the reader into believing that those examples constitute the bulk of nonprofit organizations to which MBO has been applied. The number of examples could be expanded considerably. For instance, MBO has been applied in the U.S. National Park Service, the Bureau of Outdoor Recreation, the U.S. Navy Supply Systems Command, and the mayor's office of the city of Sapporo, Japan. Nursing homes, churches, and child-care centers all have embraced MBO, as have many other nonprofit organizations. On the basis of the experience to date, it appears only logical that nonprofit applications will accelerate.

18

The Future:
Its Challenge
and Its Promise

MBO is not a panacea for nonprofit organizations—or for any other organization. However, it does have much to recommend it to any organization interested in improving the effectiveness of its managers and, through their combined effectiveness, the effectiveness of the entire organization.

No attempt is made here to recommend that all nonprofit entities adopt MBO. Such a recommendation would be shortsighted indeed. It could be made only after an exhaustive analysis of the organization, its managers, their competence and motivation, and the environment in which the organization operates.

It is definitely recommended, however, that these entities give full consideration to exploring the possible benefits that MBO could bring to them. There are compelling reasons for nonprofit organizations to take a good, hard look at MBO. These reasons can be generally grouped into five broad categories:

1. The increasing demand for greater accountability.
2. The demand for a greater voice by managers.

3. The increasing rate of change.
4. The increasing degree of complexity.
5. The dramatic increase in the number, size, and influence of nonprofit organizations and managers.

Demand for Accountability

The demand for accountability on the part of managers has never been greater. Both the marketplace and the owners are increasingly demanding more of business managers. Managers of churches and other religious institutions are being required more often to justify to their congregations the effectiveness with which stewardship is being met. Citizens, taxpayers, and organized pressure groups are demanding that government agencies and departments achieve meaningful, worthwhile goals. Students and parents alike are exerting comparable pressures on school managers and administrators. Volunteer groups are being required to document the reason for their existence. Fund-raising organizations are no longer being supported blindly just because their cause is honorable. Social agencies in general are discovering that appreciable demands are being made upon them for accountability. And now even the military finds itself in the position of having its objectives and performance questioned from many quarters.

MBO can be a potent means of helping meet this increasing demand for accountability and the challenge it poses. First, it is a means of aligning the efforts of all managers to achieve the desired ends that have been agreed upon. It helps organizations concentrate on important matters rather than getting bogged down in the routine, which serves only to dissipate efforts and resources and leaves the organization subject to criticism for following wasteful practices.

Secondly, MBO provides the nonprofit organization with concrete means for dramatizing the contributions it has made. It is able to point out what it intended to achieve (its objectives), and later it can demonstrate the results it actually achieved as compared against its objectives. This helps the nonprofit organization achieve one of its most crying needs—the need for credibility by its supporters. It can also go far to at least minimizing the often unfair stereotyping of nonprofit managers; namely, that they are inefficient, ineffective, and lacking in the competence and motivation required of their counterparts in the private sector.

Demand for Greater Voice

The plight of managers—especially middle managers—has been all but overlooked in the rush to define and treat the problem at the worker level. So far, most attention has been devoted to providing workers with more ways of gaining a greater voice in determining their futures. The same indicators used to gauge the magnitude of the problem among workers (for example, turnover, absenteeism, apathy, lack of decision-making opportunities, and a lessening opportunity to demonstrate individuality) are equally appropriate when addressing attention to managers. These indicators show that a major problem exists in the ranks of managers.

Study after study and case after case are proving that there is a potentially dangerous and costly excess of unrest and disenchantment among managers, particularly middle managers. Absenteeism, a problem traditionally associated with nonmanagement employees, is now soaring in the middle management ranks. Managerial productivity is down. One large U.S. corporation even found it necessary to conduct a special productivity improvement program for its upper-level managers. Turnover, another problem usually associated with nonmanagerial employees, is exacting a costly toll in the ranks of managers. Many are leaving business to teach, to enter public service, or to pursue other forms of endeavor where they can be their own boss or pursue their own interests.[1]

An HEW report cites additional evidence that increasing numbers of the 4.5 million middle managers in the United States are seeking a midcareer change. The report states:

> Characteristically, middle managers perceive that they lack influence on organization decision making, yet they must implement company policy—and often without sufficient authority or resources to effectively carry it out.[2]

A survey conducted recently by the Life Extension Institute in New York and quoted by Dale Tarnowieski found that "compared with 1958 figures, only one-sixth the number of middle management executives are satisfied with their jobs."[3] Tarnowieski goes on to quote from a research report prepared by the American Management Associations entitled "Manager Unions." The report surveyed middle- and lower-level managers in more than 500 U.S. organizations. He quotes:

[1] *Dun's*, August 1972.

[2] *Work in America* (Washington, D.C.: Department of Health, Education, and Welfare, 1972), p. 36.

[3] "Middle Managers' New Values," *Personnel*, January–February 1973, p. 48.

If these survey results are a valid representation of what's on management's mind, there is today widespread disenchantment among American middle managers with the prevailing state of corporate affairs. This disenchantment is largely the product of the dramatic changes in life-styles throughout American society, of a painful and prolonged recession, and of increased external pressures for business and organizational reform. . . . Economic and social insecurity is at the heart of the manager's discontent, and the leaders of American business will be treading on thin ice if they ignore or deny the possibility of a revolt in the ranks of middle management.[4]

Among other findings, the same AMA report found that three out of four of the intermediate managers surveyed admitted to a substantial increase in recent years in on-the-job frustration and general discontent. Furthermore, 18 percent of the middle managers surveyed would join a manager's union today if the law or corporate climate permitted. An additional 17 percent would seriously consider union membership as a means of strengthening what they see as a fading middle-management voice in corporate and organizational affairs.

A newer research report, *The Changing Success Ethic*, prepared for AMA and also quoted by Tarnowieski, adds additional dimension to the unrest among middle management. This report found that 35 percent of the more than 2,800 respondents at all managerial levels indicated that there was an occupational field other than business management in which they would rather be engaged. Among middle managers, nearly 44 percent envisaged an alternate career for themselves, and 70 percent of these managers expected to search for a way to make a career change in the near future.[5]

All these indications of managerial unrest should act as a positive incentive for companies to conduct a searching reexamination of their approaches to job enrichment. This examination should lead to answers and a positive program of action to cope with the following questions:

1. What is the real locus of the job enrichment problem?
2. Are job enrichment efforts being directed to this priority?
3. How can managers be expected to enrich the jobs of their employees when they themselves often are in need of job enrichment (lack of motivation)?
4. How can one who hasn't experienced enrichment in his

[4] AMACOM, 1972.
[5] AMACOM, 1973.

own job know how to practice it for others (lack of experience)?

Fortunately, MBO has pointed the way to several practical, effective ways for enriching the manager's job. It has within its total system the built-in vehicle and latitude for allowing the manager a major voice in determining both his day-to-day actions and his long-term future. It enables him to experience the attributes that contribute to job enrichment.

Viable objectives to be sought in managerial job enrichment should center around the following attributes to which one writer has referred as the "eight selfs." [6]

Self-commitment. The manager who has a major voice in setting his own objectives will be more committed to making them become a reality.

Self-motivation. As with self-commitment, the manager will strive harder to achieve his own goals.

Self-planning. When a manager knows the results he must achieve, he can plan for them.

Self-supervision. The goal-oriented manager requires less close supervision.

Self-discipline. The manager who is working with objectives and has feedback on performance tends to discipline himself.

Self-management. The manager has considerable freedom to manage his own resources to reach his objectives.

Self-development. Challenging objectives challenge the manager to more effective performance and promote his growth.

Self-reward. Meaningful rewards result from achievement and increased competency.

These, then, are the major end results that should flow from endeavors to enrich the manager's job. Working in combination and concert, they should raise the manager to the status of "entrepreneur" or "chief executive officer" of his own smaller company within the larger organization.

Probably the greatest evidence of the value of MBO as a job enricher is the vast number of top executives and middle- and lower-level managers actually working under a smoothly functioning MBO system who maintain that the most effective tool for job

---

[6] James J. Cribbin, *Effective Managerial Leadership*, AMACOM, 1972, p. 180.

enrichment is management by objectives, properly practiced! MBO has built into the system the means for accomplishing all eight of these "selfs."

Increasing Rate of Change

The continually accelerating rate of change in the world and the environment in which organizations must operate is another strong argument for a thorough study of the advisability of adopting MBO. The president of a noted school of engineering recently summarized this rate of change when he stated that everything that would be taught to the entering freshmen would be obsolete by the time they graduated. Others estimate that more change has taken place in the past ten years than took place in all the years since our country was founded.

By any measure, the rate of change has been phenomenal, and it is increasing geometrically. What was new yesterday will be old tomorrow.

Given this rate of change, no one person, or even several, can hope to successfully cope with it. What is clearly needed is the full utilization of all members of an organization—each having a segment of the entity for which he is responsible, each staying current with the changes that impact on his organization, and each constituting a change agent within his sphere of operation.

In a very real sense, MBO is a change system. It is a system designed to require the continuing review of the priorities of the organization. As these priorities change, MBO requires that objectives, plans, and budgets be changed accordingly. Thus utilizing a system that addresses itself to change, and also fully utilizing all key personnel in effecting necessary change, is an excellent means of coping with it.

Increasing Complexity

Closely allied to the rate of change is the increasing rate of complexity involved in realizing optimum results for an organization. No long-winded treatise is necessary to convince the non-profit manager that his is not a simple job.

The vast multiplicity of services provided by organizations such as the Department of Health, Education, and Welfare is a good example. The services offered by this department—approximately $120 billion per year of them—truly range from alpha to omega, from programs designed to lower the dropout rate in schools to assistance to migratory workers and their families.

Added to this are the many interested parties who do their level best to influence the department's actions—senators, congressmen, and others with special interests. Add the lobbyists, the do-gooders, and the interests of the recipients.

Then add to these the number of persons and organizations having a part in administering the department's programs. Among these are federal agencies, state governments and agencies, and third-party reimbursement groups.

To all of this must be added the changes and increased complexity of the very services the department must deliver. Take, for example, the changing roles and methods of education, the dramatic advances in medicine, and the multiplying number of welfare programs and recipients in an era of providing some type of aid for practically everyone.

In light of all of the above, it's a small wonder that the biggest problem facing HEW is the ordering of realistic priorities and the allocation of resources to them.

Once more, one of the more promising approaches to coping with this complexity is a management system that helps order priorities, and then gets all managers involved in helping cope with complexity and change. Again, no few people can hope to deal with this complexity. However, and obviously, the answer doesn't lie in merely throwing more people into the action. Only with a system like MBO can we be as sure as possible that additional numbers are needed and of the contribution they must make.

Increase in Numbers and Size

Earlier I cited the dramatic increase in the sheer weight of numbers in the nonprofit sector—increases in the numbers of managers, the increasing number of nonprofit organizations per se, the increasing proportion of the gross national product that they account for, and the increasing influence they are exerting on our daily lives. The size factor will not be further labored upon here.

It should suffice to say that these increases place an even heavier premium on following the very best and latest in management approaches. A management system such as MBO, which has been increasingly proved over a 20-year period, presents itself as a most logical candidate for consideration.

A Fork in the Road

Clearly, nonprofit organizations have come to a fork in their road. Which road they take is all-important to their future, and the choice is largely up to them.

They can adopt a "problem orientation" or an "objective orientation" in their deliberations regarding the possible adoption of MBO. The difference is illustrated by a case I recently encountered in a large municipal government organization. While the subject was different, the issue is the same.

A city manager of a large Midwest city received a proposal that would save the city several thousand dollars each year if it could be successfully implemented and administered. He called his top managers and administrators together to discuss the proposal. He soon found that his people lined up into two rather distinct groups. The essence of the thinking of the two groups was:

Group 1. Too many problems were involved in implementing the proposal. Several work procedures would have to be changed. Employees would have to be trained. The union representing the municipal employees might file grievances. Other disruptions would occur in the office. The proposal should be rejected.

Comment. This is a problem-oriented group; they first look at problems rather than at potential benefits. (Undoubtedly, they would reject any consideration of MBO out of hand.)

Group 2 The proposal seemed to have many benefits, not the least of which was the potential savings. The proposal should be investigated.

Comment. This group is objective-oriented. They first examine the issues before going to the problems. They don't let the real or imagined problems make the decision for them prematurely.

Obviously, the adoption of MBO in many nonprofit organizations won't be easy. It never is. There will be many problems that must be overcome and adaptations that must be made. But one of the primary jobs of a manager in any organization is to solve problems, not to walk away from them. The latter constitutes abdication and doesn't require very much competence, decision-making ability, or guts.

Hopefully, the vast majority of the managers of nonprofit organizations who read this book will be thoroughly receptive to:

Fully exploring the potential benefits of a well-proven management system like MBO.

Having an objective rather than a problem orientation.

Matching MBO to the requirements and circumstances of their organizations.

Determining, realistically, what aspects of MBO can and should be adopted.

Before making the decision to implement, determining how fast and how far they want to and can go with MBO.

Recognizing that with most nonprofit organizations that are starving for better management, even a half a loaf is better than none. They won't become disgruntled if they can't realize the full benefits of MBO—benefits that they might be able to realize in private-sector companies.

I fervently hope that all nonprofit organizations will accept the challenge that there's always a better way of managing.

Supplemental Training and Reference Materials

Films

Defining the Manager's Job, featuring John Humble, 28 minutes.
Available from: The Bureau of National Affairs, Inc.
5615 Fishers Lane
Rockville, Md. 20852
Theme: Explanation of the MBO system, the selection of key results areas, and setting objectives.

Business, Behaviorism, and the Bottom Line, 28 minutes.
Available from: CRM Productions
9263 West 3rd St.
Beverly Hills, Calif. 90210
Theme: The importance and application of feedback in improving managerial performance.

The Nuts and Bolts of Performance Appraisal, by Joe Batten, 28 minutes.
    Available from: The Bureau of National Affairs, Inc.
                     5615 Fishers Lane
                     Rockville, Md. 20852
    Theme: How to appraise managers, with emphasis on appraising by objectives.

Cassettes

Management by Objectives, by George S. Odiorne.
    Available from: COMCOR
                     635 Langdon St.
                     Madison, Wis. 53703
                     Telephone, toll-free: 800/356-8052
    Content: The use and applications of MBO.

Training Inventories

"Management Inventory on Management by Objectives," by Dale D. McConkey.
    Available from: Dale D. McConkey Associates
                     P.O. Box 1746
                     Madison, Wis. 53701
    Content: Sixty questions on MBO, plus answer sheets, and a manual for administering the inventory.

Bibliography

Alexander, J. W., *Managing Our Work*. Downers Grove, Ill.: Inter-varsity Press, 1972.

Batten, J. D., *Beyond Management by Objectives*. AMACOM, 1966.

Baum, Bernard, *Decentralization of Authority in a Bureaucracy*. New York: Prentice-Hall, 1960.

Clark, J. V., "Motivation in Work Groups: A Tentative View," in Costello, T. W., and Zalkind, S. S., *Psychology in Administration*. Englewood Cliffs, N.J.: Prentice-Hall, 1963, pp. 61–63.

Costello, T. W., and Zalkind, S. S., *Psychology in Administration*. Englewood Cliffs, N.J.: Prentice-Hall, 1963, p. 98.

Doh, Joon Chien, *The Planning-Programming-Budgeting System in Three Federal Agencies*. The Ford Foundation and the University of Malaya, September 1971.

Drucker, P. F., *Managing for Results*. New York: Harper & Row, 1964.

Filley, Alan C., and House, Robert J., *Managerial Process and Organizational Behavior*. Glenview, Ill.: Scott, Foresman and Company, 1969.

Goodenough, Ward Hunt, *Cooperation in Change*. New York: Russell Sage Foundation, 1963.

Herzberg, F., *Work and the Nature of Man*. New York: The World Publishing Co., 1966.

Herzberg, F., Mausner, B., and Snyderman, B. B., *The Motivation to Work*. 2d ed. New York: Wiley & Sons, Inc., 1959.

Hughes, C. L., *Goal Setting: Key to Individual and Organizational Effectiveness*. AMACOM, 1965.

Humble, John W., *Management by Objectives*. London: Management Publications Limited for the British Institute of Management, 1972.
————, *Management by Objectives in Action*. London: McGraw-Hill, 1970.
Kaplan, A., *The Conduct of Inquiry*. San Francisco: Chandler Publishing Co., 1964, pp. 128–130.
Likert, R., in Whyte, W. H. *The Organization Man*. New York: Penguin, 1956.
Linowes, David F., *Strategies for Survival*. AMACOM, 1973.
Maslow, A. H., *Motivation and Personality*. New York: Harper & Bros., 1954.
Massey, R. J., *A Concept for Progress Management*. Washington, D.C.: Naval Supply Systems Command, 1966.
McConkey, Dale D., *How to Manage by Results*. AMACOM, 1967.
————, *Planning Next Year's Profits*. AMACOM, 1968.
————, *Updating the Management Process*. AMACOM, 1971.
————, *Management by Objectives for Staff Managers*. New York: Vantage Press, 1972.
————, *No-Nonsense Delegation*, AMACOM, 1974.
McGregor, D. M., *The Human Side of Enterprise*. New York: McGraw-Hill Book Co., 1960.
Meyer, Marshall W., *Bureaucratic Structure and Authority Coordination and Control in 254 Government Agencies*. New York: Harper & Row, 1972.
Miller, E. C., *Objectives and Standards: An Approach to Planning and Control* (Research Study). AMACOM, 1966.
Nadler, Gerald, *Work Design: A Systems Concept*. Rev. ed. Homewood, Ill.: Richard D. Irwin, 1970.
Odiorne, G. S. *Management by Objectives*. New York: Pitman Publishing Co., 1965.
Redfern, G. B., *How To Evaluate Teaching*. Worthington, Ohio: School Management Institute, 1972.
Scanlan, B. K., *Results Management in Action*. Cambridge, Mass.: Management Center of Cambridge, 1967.
Schleh, E. C., *Management by Results*. New York: McGraw-Hill, 1961.
School Management Institute, *Manual on Appraisal of Teaching Performance With Self-Appraisal Instrument*. Worthington, Ohio: School Management Institute, 1971.
Stewart, N., *Strategies of Managing for Results*. New York: Parker Publishing Co., 1966.
Valentine, R. F., *Performance Objectives for Managers*. AMACOM, 1966.
Wilensky, H., "Human Relations in the Work-Place," in Arensberg, C. et al., eds. *Research in Industrial Human Relations*. New York: Harper & Row, 1957, p. 25.

Key Terms in
Management by Objectives

Accountability. The specific objectives of the manager. The specific results that must be achieved within the "responsibility."

Activity. The tasks or actions taken to secure a result. They usually are inputs rather than outputs, usually are means rather than ends. Plans often are activity-oriented, but in plans all activities are prioritized and aimed toward a desired result.

Budget. Quantification of the objectives and plans and allocation of the resources to objectives and plans.

Feedback. The information and data required by each manager to (1) write effective objectives and plans, (2) monitor their progress while they are being carried out, and (3) measure accomplishment after the action is completed.

Goal. When distinguished from "objectives," is usually defined as a longer-term, broader statement of intent; for example, "provide higher-quality services to students." Often referred to as a sense of direction.

Horizontal compatibility. When objectives and plans are blended and balanced with those of the manager's associates across the organization.

Input. The actions or methods taken to secure the output.

Joint objective. An end result requiring action by two or more managers.

Measure. The definition or delineation of the means by which accomplishment of the objective will be measured.

Mission. The reason or purpose for the organization's existence. Can be applied to an entire organization or a unit of it.

Objective. The specific end result expected from a manager and the time at which it will be achieved—the "what," "when," and "who."

Output. The end results being sought.

Plan. The "how to," the steps or ways and means by which the objective is to be achieved. Often termed "programming an objective."

Priority. A weighing of objectives and/or plans to determine the relative importance of each—which is the most important, which should be done first, which is deserving of the greater allocation of resources.

Project. Often, but not always, a project comprises short-term objectives (often two to three months in duration) covering a narrower, more specific result. For example, the lowest-level managers in an organization frequently have a greater number of objectives and objectives that are project-oriented.

Responsibility. The scope or parameters of the job; for example, all personnel functions.

Result. The actual achievement as compared to the objective. Should be expressed as an output rather than as an input.

Results evaluation. An evaluation of a manager based on the results he or she actually achieves compared to the objectives for which he or she is accountable.

Stretch. The degree by which an objective requires the manager to achieve above "average" effort or above a "routine as usual" level.

Target period. The period of time covered by the objective, the date by which the result must be achieved.

Vertical compatibility. When objectives and plans are blended and balanced with those of associates above and below the manager.

Index

routine, 55
specific, 56, 78, 140–142
updating of, 58
vertical and horizontal compatibility in, 58–59
weasel words in, 56
wording of, 59
writing of, 53–59
objective-setting process, 44–51, 54
link-pin concept in, 48
lower-level objectives in, 47–48
at lowest level, 48–49
mission statement in, 176
recommendations in, 49–50
in Renewal by Objectives, 174–182
sequence in, 53
top-level objectives in, 46–47
Occupational Health and Safety Act, 56
Office of Education, U.S., 131
Office of Regional Operations, Public Health Service, 116, 124
operational feedback, components of, 66–72
see also feedback
organization
humanistic ideals in, 187
nonprofit, see nonprofit organization
organizational clarity, in implementation process, 108
organization size, as implementation factor, 101–102
organization structure, in implementation, 102
outside consultants, in implementation process, 101, 106, 108–110

papermill, creation of, 87–88
people, as individuals, 187
performance evaluation, 74–81

alternative approach to, 81
appraisal forms in, 75–76
defects in, 75–76
evaluation form in, 78–79
measuring by objectives in, 76–77
in nonprofit organization, 41
rating process in, 78–81
specific objectives in, 77–78, 80
periodic reviews, omission of, 86
PHS, see Public Health Service
plans
control of, 70
role of in MBO, 14–15, 28
power, collaboration and reason in, 187
Practice of Management, The (Drucker), 133–134
priorities
failure in ordering of, 84
in nonprofit organization, 35–36
in writing of objectives, 53–54
profit motive, efficiency and, 2
"programitis," errors of, 88
program-planning-budgeting system, in Canada, 186
Public Health Service, U.S., 114–129
concurrence in, 124
future of MBO in, 128–129
organization of, 116–117
problems encountered with MBO in, 126–127
work program in, 120–123

rating process, in performance evaluation, 78–81
RBO, see Renewal by Objectives
recommendations, in objective-setting process, 49–50
refresher training, 87
Regional Health Administrator, 116, 127–128
objectives for, 121–122